FROM READING TO WRITING

COLIN WARD

Series Editor
LINDA ROBINSON FELLAG

From Reading to Writing 4

Pearson Education, 10 Bank Street, White Plains, NY 10606

I dedicate this book to my loving parents, Wendy and Brian Ward. I would also like to thank my wife, Stefanie, for being my sounding board, and my daughters, Tamsin and Erin, for always keeping me grounded. You are all my inspiration.
—CSW

Staff credits: The people who made up the *From Reading to Writing 4* team, representing editorial, production, design, and manufacturing, are Eleanor Barnes, John Barnes, Rosa Chapinal, Dave Dickey, Oliva Fernandez, Margot Gramer, Niki Lee, Françoise Leffler, Martha McGaughey, Linda Moser, Massimo Rubini, Jennifer Stem, Jane Townsend, Paula Van Ells, and Patricia Wosczyk.

Text composition: ElectraGraphics, Inc.
Text font: 11 pt New Aster
Credits: See page 193

Library of Congress Cataloging-in-Publication Data
Bonesteel, Lynn.
From reading to writing / Lynn Bonesteel . . . [et al.].
p. cm.
Includes index.
ISBN 0-13-205066-8—ISBN 0-13-612780-0—ISBN 0-13-233096-2—ISBN 0-13-158867-2 1. English language—Textbooks for foreign speakers. 2. Reading comprehension—Problems, exercises, etc. I. Title.
PE1128.B6223 2010
428.2'4—dc22

2009032265

ISBN-13: 978-0-13-158867-7 (with ProofWriter™)
ISBN-10: 0-13-158867-2 (with ProofWriter™)

ISBN-13: 978-0-13-247406-1 (without ProofWriter™)
ISBN-10: 0-13-247406-9 (without ProofWriter™)

ISBN: 0-13-158867-2 (with ProofWriter™) 4 5 6 7 8 9 10—V016—13

ISBN: 0-13-247406-9 (without ProofWriter™) 1 2 3 4 5 6 7 8 9 10—V016—13 12 11 10 09

Printed in the United States of America

Contents

(continued)

Introduction

OVERVIEW OF THE SERIES

From Reading to Writing 4 is the fourth in a four-book series that integrates reading and writing skills and strategies for English language learners. The four-book series includes:

Book 1—Beginning Level

Book 2—High Beginning Level

Book 3—Intermediate Level

Book 4—High Intermediate Level

Reciprocal Reading/Writing Integration

From Reading to Writing provides a complete sequence of high-interest, thematically connected activities that reciprocally integrate reading and writing.

- Students build competence in vocabulary and reading as they move toward writing skill development and completion of a writing assignment.
- Students study the features and language of reading texts and learn to apply them in their own writing.
- In the same way, writing is integrated into the reading process in accordance with research that suggests writing can enhance reading comprehension (Mlynarcyzk, Spack).

STRUCTURE OF THE BOOKS

Books 1–3 contain eight thematically focused units. Each unit consists of two topically related chapters, divided into two main sections—Reading *and* Writing—which are linked by a bridge section, From Reading to Writing. Book 4 is organized into nine units. Each unit consists of two thematically connected readings that have accompanying skills and practice activities and are linked by a bridge section. Each reading is also followed by a writing section.

Books 1–3

Each chapter in Books 1–3 includes:

Pre-Reading

Discussion
Vocabulary

Reading

Identifying Main Ideas and Details, Making Inferences
Reading Skill and Practice

Bridge Section—From Reading to Writing

Discussion, Vocabulary Review, Journal Writing

Writing

Writing Model or Examples
Writing Skills and Practice
Writing Assignment
Writing Process Steps

Book 4

Each unit of Book 4 includes:

Pre-Reading 1

Discussion
Vocabulary

Reading 1

Identifying Main Ideas and Details, Making Inferences
Reading and Vocabulary Skill and Practice

Bridge Section—From Reading to Writing

Discussion and Journal Writing

Pre-Reading 2

Discussion
Vocabulary

Reading 2

Identifying Main Ideas and Details, Making Inferences

Writing

Writing Model
Writing Skills and Practice
Writing Assignment
Writing Process Steps

Detailed Explanation of Parts, Books 1–3

Part 1, Reading

In the Pre-Reading section, students build schema by discussing the theme and studying key vocabulary before reading. High-interest readings and lively activities engage students as they develop vocabulary and reading skills and strategies that can be used in their own writing.

Bridge Section—From Reading to Writing

The Reflecting on the Reading activity focuses on content from the reading and how it can be applied to student writing. In some levels, a journal activity provides an opportunity for freewriting. Students use target vocabulary and explore a question from the reflection activity. Some levels also include exercises to activate vocabulary. Students are asked questions using target vocabulary and are encouraged to use their answers in the upcoming writing assignment.

Part 2, Writing

Writing models and writing skills practice allow students to hone their writing skills before they produce their own writing. In the writing assignment, students are led step-by-step through the writing process. This encourages them to gather ideas, focus and organize, and revise and edit their writing. This step-by-step process facilitates collaboration with classmates and the instructor and also promotes self-evaluation of writing.

Benefits to Students

This sequence of activities, common to Books 1–3, has at its core a set of essential competencies for pre-academic English learners that are emphasized throughout the four-book series. Upon completion of the activities, students will be prepared to:

- Recognize and produce a variety of sentences to express ideas (Books 1–2)
- Recognize and utilize the steps in the writing process to produce a composition (Books 2–4)
- Use ideas and language gained from reading in writing and speaking (Books 1–4)

- Organize and write a composition with a main idea and supporting ideas (Books 1–4)
- Recognize and use connectors and other devices that show relationships among ideas in texts (Books 1–4)
- Recognize and express the main idea and supporting details of a reading (Books 1–4)

Vocabulary Focus

The *From Reading to Writing* series also features a strong focus on vocabulary development. The high-frequency vocabulary targeted in each book is derived from three highly recognized vocabulary lists:

- West's *General Service List* (1953) of the 2,000 most frequently used words in English
- Coxhead's *Academic Word List* (2000) of the 570 most common word families
- Dilin Liu's list of most common idioms (2003)

Vocabulary experts agree that academic-bound students who acquire the words on the West and Coxhead lists will know more than 90 percent of the words they will encounter in academic texts (Nation, 2000). Furthermore, research studies have shown that repeated exposure to new words, and application of new vocabulary in writing and speech, increase the chances that students will acquire the target words (N. Schmitt, Nation, Laufer).

From Reading to Writing stresses vocabulary acquisition by providing opportunities for students to encounter, study, and use new words in each of these sections of a chapter or unit:

- Pre-Reading vocabulary activities
- Reading
- From Reading to Writing bridge section
- Post-Reading vocabulary review

Writing Resources

A full complement of appendices serves as resources for student writers. These include a section on Avoiding Plagiarism; a Grammar Reference; a Correction Symbols chart, which presents commonly used correction marks; a Vocabulary Review for each reading; and an alphabetized Word List of target vocabulary, organized by reading and unit. Additionally, an online e-rater allows students to submit their compositions and receive prompt, individualized feedback.

References

Coxhead, A. (2000). "A New Academic Word List." *TESOL Quarterly*, 34(2), 213–38.

Laufer, B. (2003). "Vocabulary Acquisition in a Second Language: Do Learners Really Acquire Most Vocabulary by Reading?" *Canadian Modern Language Review* 59, 4: 565–585.

Liu, Dilin. (2003). "The Most Frequently Used Spoken American English Idioms: A Corpus Analysis and Its Implications." *TESOL Quarterly* 37, 671–700.

Mlynarcyzk, Rebecca. (1993). "Conversations of the Mind: A Study of the Reading/Writing Journals of Bilingual College Students." Diss. New York U, *DAI* 54, 4004A.

Nation, I. S. P. (2001). *Learning Vocabulary in Another Language.* Cambridge: Cambridge University Press.

Schmitt, N. (2000). *Vocabulary in Language Teaching.* Cambridge: Cambridge University Press.

Schmitt, N. & McCarthy, M. (Eds.). (1997). *Vocabulary: Description, Acquisition, and Pedagogy.* Cambridge: Cambridge University Press.

Spack, Ruth. (1993). "Student Meets Text, Text Meets Student: Finding a Way into Academic Discourse." *Reading in the Composition Classroom: Second Language Perspectives.* Joan G. Carson and Ilona Leki (Eds.). Boston: Heinle, 183–96.

Scope and Sequence

Unit		Reading	Reading Skill	Vocabulary Skill	Writing Skill	Writing Assignment
1	Inventions	1 – *A Zone in Time*	Skimming for main ideas	Using adjective-noun collocations	Organizing the parts of an essay	Writing an essay about an invention
		2 – *The Remarkable Clarence Birdseye*			Topic sentences and supporting sentences	
2	Careers	1 – *How Networking Works*	Recognizing time and sequence markers	Using idioms with *get*	Organizing the process essay	Writing a process essay about careers
		2 – *How to Run a Successful Business*			Writing an effective introduction	
3	The Environment	1– *Can Cell-Phone Recycling Help African Gorillas?*	Recognizing coherence markers	Using a dictionary	Organizing the problem-solution essay	Writing a problem-solution essay about the environment
		2 – *The Water Beneath Our Feet*			Writing the conclusion	

Unit		Reading	Reading Skill	Vocabulary Skill	Writing Skill	Writing Assignment
4	Fact or Fiction?	1 – *Lucky Charms*	Annotating a reading	Using collocations with *do* and *make*	Writing a summary	Writing a summary of an article
		2 – *Legendary Creatures*				
5	Personality	1 – *Musical Personalities*	Recognizing classification markers	Using verb suffixes	Organizing the classification essay	Writing a classification essay about people or feelings
		2 – *Eustress or You Stress?*				
6	Gender	1 – *Shopping by the Sexes*	Using a Venn Diagram	Using adverb-adjective collocations	Organizing the comparison-contrast essay	Writing a comparison-contrast essay about gender
		2 – *Fashionable Men*			Using comparison and contrast markers	

Unit		Reading	Reading Skill	Vocabulary Skill	Writing Skill	Writing Assignment
7	Human Nature	1 – *Why You Can't Turn Away*	Recognizing a causal chain	Understanding Latin prefixes	Organizing the cause-effect essay	Writing a cause-effect essay about an aspect of human nature
		2 – *To Laugh Is Human*			Using cause-effect markers	
8	Privacy	1 – *Future with Nowhere to Hide*	Identifying arguments and counter-arguments	Using noun suffixes	Organizing the argumentative essay	Writing an argumentative essay about technology
		2 – *More Parents Going High-Tech to Track Kids*				
9	Literature	1 – *The Model Millionaire (Part 1)*	Recognizing themes in literature	Identifying formal and informal synonyms	Organizing the thematic analysis essay	Writing a thematic analysis essay on a piece of literature
		2 – *The Model Millionaire (Part 2)*				

UNIT

1

Inventions

In this unit you will:

- read articles about the inventions of time zones and frozen food
- learn strategies for skimming texts
- organize and write an essay

PRE-READING 1

Discussion

Discuss the questions in pairs or small groups.

1. Name an old or modern invention that benefits many people. How has this invention helped people in their daily lives?
2. List these inventions in chronological (time) order, from oldest to newest: the typewriter, the Internet, the telephone, the thermometer, and the automobile.

Vocabulary

Read the sentences. Match the boldfaced words with the definitions in the box.

c 1. There is an **underlying** assumption that the Internet was invented to benefit all people, but it was actually first created to help scientists only.

d 2. The dictionary offers a **systematic** way to look up words and definitions because it is arranged alphabetically.

e 3. When companies create a new product, they must **take into account** how much it will cost to make. They must also consider whether people will want to buy it.

h 4. The first movies were silent. Later, when technology improved, sound was **incorporated** into movies to make them more entertaining.

i 5. The most **prominent** building in Paris is the Eiffel Tower. You can see it from miles away.

g 6. Henry Ford made all of his Model T cars have a **uniform** size and shape. As a result, they all looked similar.

b 7. Alexander Graham Bell's invention of the telephone has **fostered** easier communication between people.

a 8. Making a long-distance phone call requires connections over an **extensive** system of telephone lines over thousands of miles.

j 9. France was the first country to **implement** the metric system in 1795. Today, 95 percent of the world uses the metric system.

f 10. Black and white televisions were very popular when they were first produced. **Nonetheless**, color televisions eventually replaced them in most homes.

a. very large in size, amount, or degree
b. help develop a skill, feeling, idea, etc. over a period of time
c. very basic or important, but not necessarily easily noticed
d. organized carefully and done thoroughly
e. consider or include particular facts or details when making a decision or judgment about something
f. in spite of what has just been mentioned
g. the same in all of its parts or among all of its members
h. include as part of a group, system, plan, etc.
i. large and easy to see
j. begin to make a plan, process, etc. happen

Skimming for Main Ideas

Skimming means reading a text very quickly to identify main ideas. When readers skim, they don't need to know every detail in the text. They are only looking for the most important information. Students often need to skim when they take timed reading exams or are preparing for an essay or research paper.

Use these steps to skim a text:

- **Read the title and any subtitles.**
- **Read the first and last paragraph.**
- **Read the first sentence of all the middle paragraphs.**

Practice

Skim the reading "A Zone in Time." Then answer the questions.

1. What is the main idea of the article? Circle the letter of the best answer.

   a. the Egyptian sundial

   b. the differences between old and new clocks

   c. the history behind time zones

2. Which paragraphs discuss these main ideas? Write the number of the paragraph next to each idea.

   __2__ a. how the Egyptians measured time

   ____ b. why European cities used to be on different times

   ____ c. why the railroad made time more important

   ____ d. why Sir Sandford Fleming invented time zones

   ____ e. how time zones have changed the world

READING 1

A Zone in Time

1 *Time flies. Time is money. Time is of the essence.*[1] Humans are so obsessed[2] with the concept of time that the world itself seems to "tick." Today, there is an **underlying** assumption that everyone in the world arranges activities according to the same 24-hour period. The idea of a standardized[3] time, however, is a relatively modern concept. Years ago, people living in the same country, or even the same town, did not necessarily follow the same time. In fact, it took thousands of years for people to discover a way to measure this thing we call "time."

2 The concept of measuring time began with the Egyptians in 3500 B.C.E. The Egyptians were fascinated by the science behind the sun and stars and wanted to measure the passing of time in a **systematic** way. They placed a tall, pointed stone in a location that received continuous sunlight, and followed the shadow of the stone to determine the time of day. They used "noon" or "midday" to describe the time of day when the shadow was longest. The result was the world's very first sundial.

3 In the years that followed, people began using marks on a circle to divide the shadows into separate hours. However, despite these improvements, sundials were still not very precise. They did not **take into account** that the amount of sunlight could vary depending on the time of year. Moreover, they could not indicate the passing of the nighttime hours.

4 About five thousand years after the invention of the sundial, the Italian inventor Galileo began to experiment with the pendulum.[4] In 1656, Dutch mathematician and astronomer Christiaan Huygens used this new invention and **incorporated** it into his design for the first mechanical clock. Finally, time became more accurate. Now, unlike the ancient Egyptians, people could easily count minutes and even seconds both during the day and at night.

5 Pendulum clocks appeared all over major European cities in the early 1800s, but they were usually on different times. Elaborate clocks were placed on **prominent** buildings in cities and towns, and local townspeople depended on the bell of the clock tower to know when each hour had passed. However, each town had to make its own best guess of when the sun was at its highest peak, or 12 noon. Consequently, local time for one town was often different from the time in a neighboring town.

6 Not having a **uniform** time for all towns did not cause problems initially. In the early 1800s, people did not have regular contact with other cities and towns, so there was no need to standardize a national time. But when the railroad appeared during the Industrial Revolution,[5] everything changed.

[1] **time is of the essence:** used to say that it is important to do something as quickly as possible
[2] **obsess:** think about something all the time so that you cannot think of anything else
[3] **standardize:** make all of one particular type, the same as each other
[4] **pendulum:** a long stick or string with a weight at the bottom that swings regularly from side to side, especially in a large clock
[5] **Industrial Revolution:** the period in the 18th and 19th centuries in Europe when machines and factories began to be used to produce goods in large quantities

7 Trains **fostered** more contact between cities and towns than ever before. But because towns operated at different local times, travelers had to reset their watches when they arrived at a new city. Furthermore, train schedules could not be synchronized[6] because each town's official time was different. This caused much confusion for travelers, who often missed their trains.

8 The solution to this problem came from Sir Sandford Fleming and his invention of time zones. Fleming was a railway engineer who created the first **extensive** system of railroads in eastern Canada. Because he was in the railroad business, Fleming wanted to **implement** a worldwide standard time to keep all cities and countries synchronized. Since the sun circles the earth every 24 hours, Fleming wanted to divide the world into 24 separate time zones. He also wanted to create a prime meridian, or a location where time would begin each day.

9 Fleming proposed his ideas to the International Meridian Conference in 1884. The conference viewed Fleming's ideas with some skepticism.[7] **Nonetheless**, it agreed to designate the longitude of Greenwich, England, as the prime meridian since many British railway companies were already using Greenwich mean time (GMT) as their standard time. However, it took a while for all countries to adopt Fleming's time zones. By 1895, American states began to abide by[8] the Pacific, mountain, central, and eastern time zones. However, it was not until 1918 that the United States government passed the Standard Time Act to make the use of time zones mandatory for the entire nation.

10 Today, Fleming's time zones have become the standard for measuring time all around the world. Thanks to his invention, people no longer have to guess what time it is. Travelers and businesspeople know that when it is 12:00 P.M. in New York, it will be 5:00 P.M. in London and 2:00 A.M. in Tokyo. So, the next time you catch a plane on time, give thanks to the man who made it all possible. Without the results of Fleming's ingenuity,[9] you could be waiting at the gate for a very long time.

[6] **synchronize:** arrange for two or more actions to happen at exactly the same time

[7] **skepticism:** an attitude of doubt about whether something is true, right, or good

[8] **abide by:** accept and obey a decision, rule, agreement, etc., even though you may not agree with it

[9] **ingenuity:** skill at inventing things or thinking of new ideas

Identifying Main Ideas

Answer the questions.

1. How did the Egyptians measure time?
2. Why did European cities use to be on different times?
3. Why did the railroad make time more important to people?
4. Why did Sir Sandford Fleming invent time zones?
5. How have time zones changed the world?

Identifying Details

Scan (read the text quickly to find specific information) the reading on page 4. Complete each sentence with the missing information.

1. The ___Egyptians___ invented the world's first clock in 3500 B.C.E.
2. ________________ could not keep accurate time, and they did not work in the dark.
3. The railroad was invented during a period of history called the ________________ ________________.
4. The ________________ ________________ is on the longitude of Greenwich, England.
5. In 1918, the United States passed the ________________ ________________ ________________, which required all states to use Sandford Fleming's time zones.

Making Inferences

Infer what the writer would say is true even though it is not directly stated. Check (✔) each statement the writer would agree with.

__✔__ 1. The ancient Egyptians didn't know about minutes and seconds.
____ 2. The sundial was not a popular invention.
____ 3. During the early 1800s, many people had clocks in their homes.
____ 4. At first, many people believed Fleming's time zones would never work.
____ 5. Fleming proposed using time zones because they benefited him.

VOCABULARY SKILL

Using Adjective-Noun Collocations

Collocations are words that often go together, or collocate. Certain adjectives are frequently used with certain nouns to make adjective-noun collocations. For example, the adjective *heavy* can be used to describe many nouns, but not all nouns. A person can have a *heavy* influence or a *heavy* accent, but not a *heavy* pronunciation.

Practice

A. ***Scan Reading 1 and look for the adjectives in the box. Match each adjective with the noun it collocates with in the reading.***

extensive	prominent	systematic	~~underlying~~	uniform

1. ___underlying___ assumption
2. ________________ way
3. ________________ buildings
4. ________________ time
5. ________________ system

B. Complete each sentence with the correct adjective-noun collocation from the chart.

Some Adjective-Noun Collocations

underlying	factor message
systematic	error method
prominent	person part
uniform	size weight
extensive	influence amount

1. Companies do an ___extensive___ ___amount___ of research before they decide to make a new product. They talk to many people to see if they would be interested to buy it in the future.
2. Most inventors use a(n) ________________ ________________ when developing an invention. They take the process one step at a time.
3. Laptop computers don't have a(n) ________________ ________________. They can range from a few pounds to more than ten pounds.
4. Convenience was the ________________ ________________ behind the invention of supermarkets.
5. The invention of the camera had a(n) ________________ ________________ on the art world. Photography became a new art form, and many artists started to paint nonrealistic pictures.
6. Benjamin Franklin was not only a famous inventor, but he was also a(n) ________________ ________________ in early American politics.

FROM READING TO WRITING

Journal
Choose one of your answers and write a journal entry.

Reflecting on the Reading

Discuss the questions in pairs or small groups.

1. Name an invention that helps to save you time. How much time does it save you? What would your life be like if you didn't have this invention?
2. How important is it to you to be on time to an appointment or meeting? Do you believe some cultures value being on time more than others? Explain.

PRE-READING 2

Discussion

Discuss the questions in pairs or small groups.

1. Do you prefer to make your own meals? Why or why not?
2. Do you think restaurant food is better than homemade food? Explain.
3. What are some reasons that people choose to buy frozen food rather than fresh food?

Vocabulary

Read the boldfaced words and their definitions. Then complete each sentence with the correct word. Change the form of words as needed.

alteration:	a small change that makes someone or something slightly different
captivate:	attract and interest someone very much
commence:	begin or start something
commonplace:	happening or existing in many places, and therefore not special or unusual
exceed:	be more than a particular number, amount, etc.
persistent:	continuing to do something even though it is difficult or other people oppose it
reluctant:	slow and unwilling
revolutionary:	completely new and different, especially in a way that leads to great improvements
trend:	a general tendency in the way a situation is changing or developing
trigger:	make something happen

1. The automobile was a(n) ___revolutionary___ invention. It completely changed the way people moved from place to place.
2. Cartoons ___captivated___ children when they first appeared on television in the 1950s. Children were attracted to them because they saw characters come to life on the screen.
3. The production of laptop computers ___commenced___ long after desktop computers were first introduced.
4. Scientific discoveries often ___trigger___ new advances in technology, even in unrelated fields.
5. The light bulb is an invention that has had very few ___alterations___ over time. Light bulbs of the 19th century would still work in today's lamps.
6. People are sometimes ___reluctant___ to buy a brand-new invention because they worry that it won't work correctly.
7. Sunglasses became popular in the 1930s. Today, wearing sunglasses is still a very popular ___trand___ around the world.
8. It took Albert Einstein 10 years to develop his theory that $E=mc^2$. Because he was so ___persistent___, he never stopped working on it until he found the answer.
9. Scales at airports make sure that a person's baggage doesn't ___exceed___ the legal weight limit.
10. Fax machines are ___commonplace___ in many businesses. Thousands of companies use them every day.

READING 2

The Remarkable Clarence Birdseye

1 In the 1950s, Americans were glued to[1] the television. This **revolutionary** invention **captivated** American audiences and transformed the way American families spent their free time together. Television also changed the way people ate. By 1954, TV dinners—complete frozen dinners on a metal tray that could be cooked in the oven—had appeared in American grocery stores. Dinner no longer had to take time away from

(continued)

[1] **be glued to something:** look at something with all your attention

watching TV. Americans could dine while they tuned in to their favorite shows, and many did just that. In the first year that TV dinners appeared in American grocery stores, more than 10 million were sold, and since then, the frozen food business has become a multibillion dollar industry. However, the frozen foods of the 50s and today could never have existed without an even more important invention—the process of freezing food itself. It was Clarence Birdseye who was responsible for figuring out how to freeze foods so that they remained fresh and ready to eat out of the freezer.

2 Clarence Birdseye was born in 1886 in Brooklyn, New York. He showed a great interest in food at a young age when he took a cooking class in high school. After he graduated from college, Birdseye worked for the U.S. Department of Agriculture. During this time, Birdseye began eating unusual foods. He even made his own soup, which sometimes consisted of mice, rats, gophers, or chipmunks.

3 In 1912, Birdseye moved to Canada, where his relationship with frozen food **commenced**. For eight years, Birdseye traveled the cold Canadian terrain by dogsled to collect and sell animal furs. Along the way, he ate birds, polar bear, skunk, and even whale. He also consumed a lot of fish, and he soon began to notice that fish still tasted good even after it had been frozen in the snow and then thawed.[2] During his travels, Birdseye met the Inuits, a group of people who live in very cold regions of Canada. He observed that the Inuits froze fish so quickly that it kept its original flavor and texture better than fish that was slowly frozen. Watching the Inuits **triggered** Birdseye's efforts to duplicate their quick-freezing process when he moved back to the United States in 1920. His dream was to make frozen foods available to all people.

4 After six years and some **alterations** to the Inuits' freezing method, Birdseye eventually found success, inventing the first machine that could flash freeze[3] food. Because he needed a place to store these frozen foods, Birdseye also invented the first commercial freezer. Unfortunately, his inventions required a lot of money, and Birdseye was broke.[4]

5 Although many people were **reluctant** to believe that frozen food would become a major success, in 1929 Birdseye convinced the Postum Company to buy his invention for $22 million. Working for the Postum Company, Birdseye and 22 chemists created a packaging system that used cellophane[5] to cover the food cartons. The company changed the name of his food products to Birds Eye Foods, and on March 6, 1930, the first frozen foods appeared in 18 grocery stores in Springfield, Massachusetts. According to Birds Eye Foods, shoppers could choose from 27 different items, including frozen peas, spinach, raspberries, fish, and various meats.

6 The new food was not an immediate success. The items were expensive. Furthermore, grocery stores did not have freezers to store the products. They were stored in ice-cream cabinets and were not easily visible. During the 1930s, many people in the food business believed frozen foods would only be a passing **trend**.

7 But Birdseye was a very **persistent**

[2] **thaw:** become warmer and change from frozen to unfrozen

[3] **flash freeze:** freeze food quickly so that its quality is not damaged

[4] **broke:** having no money

[5] **cellophane:** thin, transparent material used for wrapping

man, and he refused to accept failure. Stores could not afford to buy freezers for frozen foods, so Birdseye invented a cheap freezer display case that stores could rent. Because he wanted to sell his foods nationwide, Birdseye rented special railroad cars to ship his company's products all across the United States. Birdseye had figured out how to make his frozen foods available to all people, and this marked the true birth of the frozen food industry. By the 1950s, frozen food sales **exceeded** $1 billion. Birdseye's invention was here to stay.

8 Today, frozen meats and vegetables have become **commonplace** in many parts of the world, from Japan to Europe to Central and South America. Birdseye's invention revolutionized the food industry, but Birdseye never saw himself as a revolutionary person. He once said, "I do not consider myself to be a remarkable person. I did not make exceptionally high grades when I went to high school. I never finished college. I am not the world's best salesman. But I am intently curious about the things which I see around me, and this curiosity, combined with a willingness to assume risks, has been responsible for such success and satisfaction as I have achieved in life."

Identifying Main Ideas

Read each question. Circle the letter of the best answer.

1. What is the main idea of the reading?
   a. Clarence Birdseye spent years inventing frozen food, which has changed the way millions of people eat.
   b. During the 1950s, watching television became very popular in American homes.
   c. Birdseye took a long time to develop frozen food, and it eventually made him poor.
   d. At first, people didn't think frozen foods would become popular because they were expensive.

2. Why was Birdseye's time in Canada so important?
   a. He tried eating many different types of unusual animals.
   b. He discovered how well frozen fish kept its original taste.
   c. He worked as a fur trader and traveled around a lot.
   d. He was forced to travel around the country by dogsled.

3. What is the main idea of paragraph 5?
   a. Birdseye's experiments with frozen food cost him a lot of money.
   b. Birdseye did not want to sell his invention to the Postum Company.
   c. Birdseye used cellophane to cover the frozen meals he created.
   d. The Postum Company helped Birdseye develop and sell his food.

4. What is the main idea of paragraph 7?
   a. Sales of Birds Eye frozen foods didn't exceed $1 billion until the 1950s.
   b. Stores weren't able to afford the freezers that Birds Eye Foods required.
   c. Railroad cars were used to transport frozen meals to grocery stores.
   d. Birdseye succeeded because he was persistent and didn't accept failure.

Identifying Details

Scan the reading on pages 9–11. Complete each sentence with the missing information.

1. Birdseye's first job was with the U.S. Department of Agriculture.
2. In 1912, Birdseye left his job and moved to Canada.
3. The Inuits are a group of people who live in very cold regions of Canada.
4. In 1929, Birdseye sold his invention to the Postum Company.
5. Sales of frozen food exceeded $1 billion by the 1950s.

Making Inferences

Infer what the writer would say is true even though it is not directly stated. Check (✔) each statement the writer would agree with.

✓ 1. Convenience is an important value in American culture.
____ 2. Birdseye didn't know whether frozen food would become popular.
✓ 3. Birdseye wanted to invent things that made people's lives easier.
____ 4. Americans buy more frozen food items than the Japanese or Chinese.
✓ 5. Birdseye did not care if his invention made him rich and famous.

FROM READING TO WRITING

> ***Vocabulary***
> For more practice with vocabulary, go to pages 174–175.

Reflecting on the Reading

Discuss the questions in pairs or small groups.

1. Which quality do you think is the most important for a successful inventor to have: intelligence, curiosity, or persistence? Choose one and explain.
2. Why do you think people are sometimes reluctant to try a new invention? Explain.
3. If you had the chance to meet either Sir Sandford Fleming or Clarence Birdseye, who would you choose? Why?

WRITING

> ***Journal***
> Choose one of your answers and write a journal entry.

Writing an Essay

An **essay** is a group of paragraphs that discusses one main topic. In this book, you will write essays with four, five, or six paragraphs. There are many different kinds of essays, but all essays have the following parts:

- **Introduction.** The introduction is the first paragraph of the essay. It introduces the topic and includes the **thesis statement**. The thesis statement is the sentence that expresses the main idea of the essay. It is usually the last sentence of the introduction.
- **Body paragraphs.** The body paragraphs are the middle paragraphs of the essay. Each body paragraph discusses one specific idea about the thesis. A body paragraph begins or ends with a topic sentence that identifies its focus. **Supporting sentences** then give details that support the paragraph's main idea.
- **Conclusion.** The conclusion is the last paragraph of the essay. It usually begins with the **restated thesis**, which summarizes the main idea of the essay. It finishes with the writer's **final thoughts** about the topic. Final thoughts reflect on what the writer has said in the essay and often leave the reader with something to think about.

Prediction

Read the model essay. Then label the paragraphs **introduction, body paragraph,** *or* **conclusion.**

MODEL

The Benefits of Smart Phones

1. ________________

THESIS STATEMENT →

Modern society has triggered the development of many new technological devices. Today, people are busier than ever before. Consequently, the trend is to develop devices that help people do many tasks at once. Smart phones can do this. A smart phone is a small handheld device that incorporates many useful features such as an electronic calendar, e-mail access, and even cell-phone capabilities. <u>Smart phones help people organize their lives and make certain tasks more convenient.</u>

TOPIC SENTENCE →

2. ________________

<u>Smart phones store and organize information very easily and efficiently.</u> They allow you to write directly on the screen so you don't have to type in the information. You can also perform a number of useful tasks with these phones. One of their best features is the electronic address book, which can store hundreds of addresses, phone numbers, and e-mail addresses. Smart phones also have a calendar that you can use to save important dates such as birthdays and anniversaries. Finally, smart phones have an appointment reminder, which tells you of upcoming appointments so you don't forget about them.

TOPIC SENTENCE →

3. ________________

<u>Smart phones are very convenient.</u> Because they are so small, you can take them anywhere you go. Many smart phones can connect to the Internet, so you can browse the Web, send e-mails, or chat with friends from any location without carrying around a big bulky computer. Smart phones are also convenient for students and businesspeople, who can use them to take notes electronically during lectures or business meetings.

RESTATED THESIS →

4. ________________

<u>Without a doubt, smart phones can make people's lives easier.</u> People are sometimes reluctant to try newer technology, but those who decide to buy these revolutionary devices will not be disappointed. They offer an extensive number of features in one easy-to-use gadget, and they will continue to get even better as technology improves.

WRITING
SKILL

Organizing the Parts of an Essay

The diagram below shows how the model essay is organized. Notice how the main idea in the **thesis statement** is supported by the ideas in the **topic sentences**. The **restated thesis** summarizes the main idea of the thesis statement in different words.

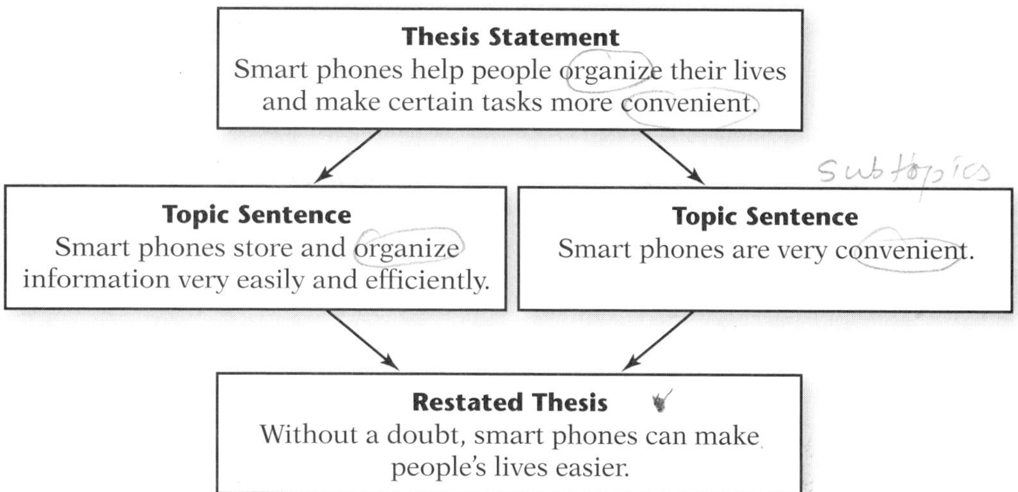
Thesis Statement
Smart phones help people organize their lives and make certain tasks more convenient.
Topic Sentence
Smart phones store and organize information very easily and efficiently.
Topic Sentence
Smart phones are very convenient.
Restated Thesis
Without a doubt, smart phones can make people's lives easier.

The thesis statement is the most important sentence of the essay. It is usually the last sentence of the introduction. A thesis statement should identify the topic, focus on one specific point about the topic, and represent a belief, observation, or attitude.

EXAMPLES

The invention of frozen foods has changed the way people eat.

Smart phones have benefited people in many ways.

A thesis statement might list the subtopics of the body paragraphs.

EXAMPLE

Smart phones help people organize their lives and make certain tasks more convenient.

A thesis statement should NOT be a known fact or announce the topic only.

EXAMPLES

Clarence Birdseye invented frozen food in the 1920s.

In this essay, I am going to discuss smart phones.

Practice

Read the pairs of sentences. Check (✔) the sentence that is a thesis statement.

1. ____ a. This essay is going to be about the invention of the television.

   ____ b. Television benefits people because it is entertaining and informative.

2. ____ a. Laptop computers can be more expensive than desktop computers, but many people buy them.

   ____ b. There are three main differences between desktop computers and laptop computers.

3. ____ a. Automobiles have affected society positively.

   ____ b. Most people in America drive an automobile.

4. ____ a. The Internet has had a positive impact on education, business, and people's personal lives.

   ____ b. I am going to write about Tim Berners-Lee, the man who invented the World Wide Web.

5. ____ a. The first digital camera that people could buy appeared in stores in 1991.

   ____ b. Digital cameras are superior to traditional cameras in three ways.

Topic Sentences and Supporting Sentences

The **topic sentence** is usually the first sentence of a body paragraph. It identifies the main idea of the body paragraph. The topic sentence is followed by **supporting sentences**. Supporting sentences include specific details that make the idea in the topic sentence more understandable for the reader.

In the second body paragraph of the model essay, notice how the supporting sentences explain the idea of the topic sentence in more detail.

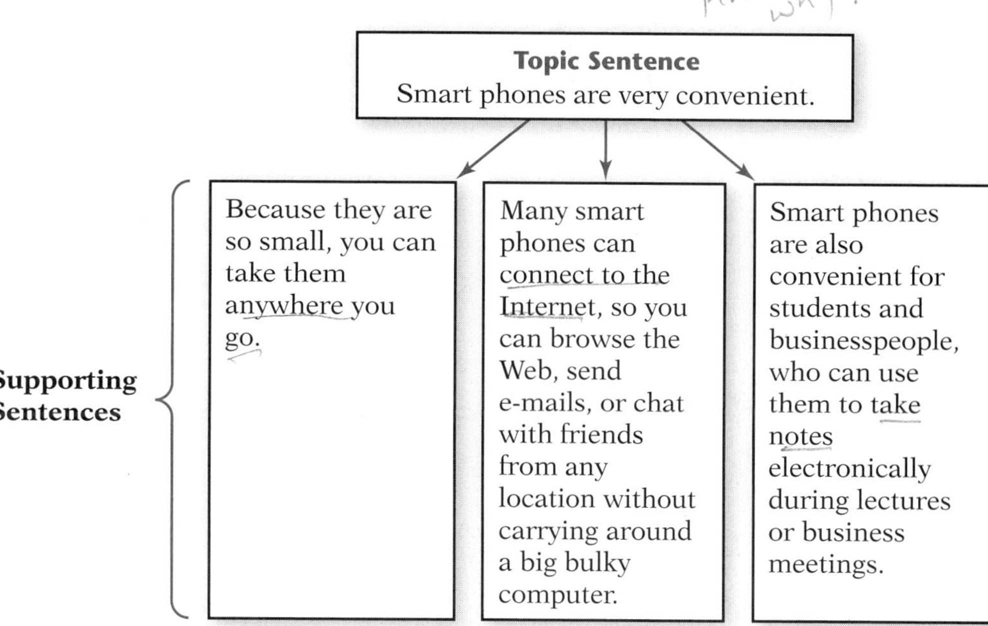

Topic Sentence
Smart phones are very convenient.
Supporting Sentences
Because they are so small, you can take them anywhere you go.
Many smart phones can connect to the Internet, so you can browse the Web, send e-mails, or chat with friends from any location without carrying around a big bulky computer.
Smart phones are also convenient for students and businesspeople, who can use them to take notes electronically during lectures or business meetings.

Practice

A. Read the thesis statement and the topic sentence. Write another topic sentence that supports the thesis statement. Then write a restated thesis.

1. Thesis statement: The invention of the automobile has greatly benefited people.
   Topic sentence: Cars help people get around town very easily.
   a. Topic sentence: *Automobiles help people save time.*
   b. Restated thesis: *People's lives have improved because of the automobile.*
2. Thesis statement: People use computers in many different ways.
   Topic sentence: Children use computers to play video games and chat with friends.
   a. Topic sentence: __________
   b. Restated thesis: __________
3. Thesis statement: People have received many benefits from the invention of the radio.
   Topic sentence: Radio stations offer many kinds of music to enjoy.
   a. Topic sentence: __________
   b. Restated thesis: __________
4. Thesis: The Internet has several important uses.
   Topic sentence: Students can use the Internet to do research for school.
   a. Topic sentence: __________
   b. Restated thesis: __________

B. ***Work in pairs or small groups. Write supporting sentences for each body paragraph.***

Television

Paragraph 1 The television is one of the most popular appliances in people's homes today. Televisions are so common in America that some people have one for every room, including the kitchen and bathroom. This invention has been around since the 1950s, but its benefits haven't changed. Thanks to television, people's lives have improved in different ways.

Paragraph 2 First of all, television helps people stay aware of what is happening in the world.

Paragraph 3 In addition, television provides many educational benefits.

Paragraph 4 The invention of the television has produced important benefits. Today, watching television has become a standard pastime for people all around the world, offering programs to match everyone's needs, from children to adults. There are many new technological devices out there today, but this is one invention that is here to stay.

WRITING ASSIGNMENT

Write an essay. Follow the steps.

STEP 1 **Get ideas.**

A. Choose a topic for your essay. Check (✔) it.

❑ **Topic 1:** Ways a specific technological service or device such as the Internet, computers, cell phones, and so forth, helps people

❑ **Topic 2:** How a popular invention in your country is used, for example, at school, at work, and/or at home

B. Brainstorm and list as many ideas about your topic as you can. Try to complete this task in five minutes or less.

C. Circle the ideas you will use in your essay.

STEP 2 Organize your ideas.

Write an outline for your essay. Use the ideas from Step 1.

Thesis statement: The invention of airplane has got many benifits to people.

Topic sentence: airplane can help people's lives who is in danger.

Topic sentence: airplane helps us to study abroad.

Restated thesis: Our lives become better than before by the invertin of airplane.

STEP 3 Write a rough draft.

A. Begin the introduction by explaining what the invention is and why it is popular. Finish with a thesis statement.

B. Begin each body paragraph with a topic sentence. Explain the idea in the topic sentence with supporting sentences that give specific details, examples, and explanations.

C. Begin the conclusion with a restated thesis. Finish by stating your opinion about the invention.

STEP 4 Revise your rough draft.

Read your essay. Use the Writing Checklist to look for mistakes. Work alone or in pairs.

Writing Checklist

- ❑ Does your introduction have a clear thesis statement that gives the topic and main idea of the essay?
- ❑ Do your body paragraphs have a clear topic sentence?
- ❑ Do your body paragraphs support your thesis statement?
- ❑ Does your conclusion have a restated thesis?
- ❑ Did you use vocabulary from the unit appropriately in your writing?
- ❑ Did you use correct essay format (adding a title, indenting paragraphs)?

STEP 5 Edit your writing.

A. Edit your essay. Use the correction symbols chart on page 173. Correct any mistakes in capitalization, punctuation, spelling, verb tense, or the use of the present perfect.

The *present perfect* is used for the indefinite (non-specific) past.

EXAMPLE

PRESENT PERFECT
have become
Computers ~~became~~ common in many American homes.

The *present perfect* also describes an action that started in the past and continues to the present.

EXAMPLE

PRESENT PERFECT
have been
Cell phones ~~are~~ popular for many years.

B. Work in pairs. Exchange essays and check each other's work.

STEP 6 Write a final copy.

Correct your mistakes. Copy your final essay and give it to your instructor.

UNIT

2

Careers

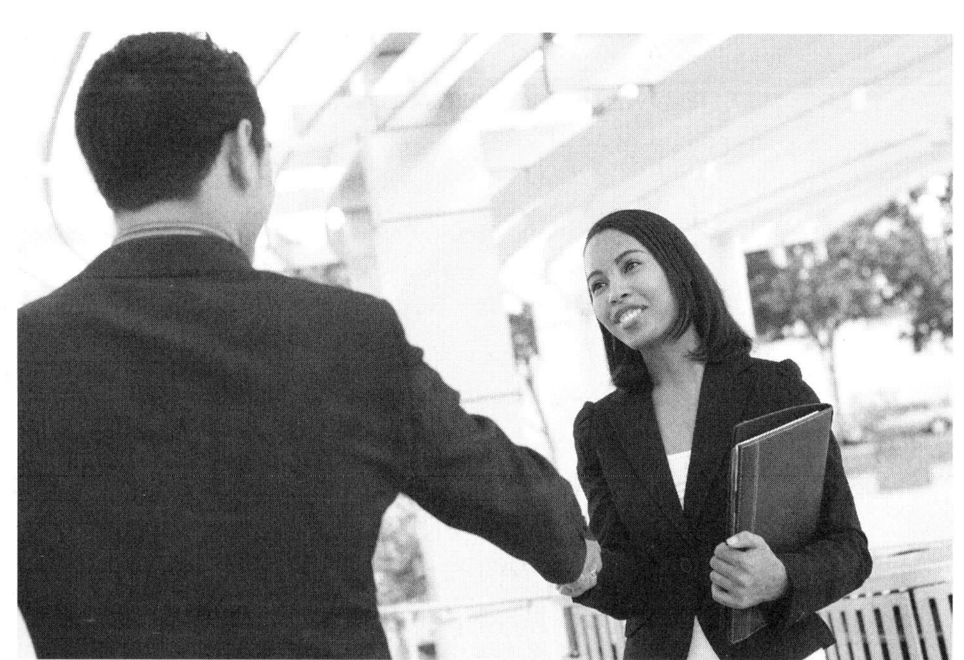

In this unit you will:

- read articles about networking and student entrepreneurs
- learn to recognize time and sequence markers
- organize and write a process essay
- learn to write an effective introduction

PRE-READING 1

Discussion

Discuss the questions in pairs or small groups.

1. How do people get good jobs?
2. What are your career goals? How will you achieve them?
3. Is it difficult for students to work and go to school at the same time? Explain.

Vocabulary

Read the sentences. Match the boldfaced words with the definitions in the box.

__f__ 1. Companies are always looking for ways to attract **potential** customers. Many use television commercials as a way to get people interested in their products.

____ 2. Jacob and Brian are **acquaintances** from work. They say hello to each other, but they don't really talk that much.

____ 3. Sonia has many business **contacts**. Some of these people have helped Sonia become more successful at her job.

____ 4. Newspapers can be excellent **sources** of information. Every week they list openings for all kinds of jobs.

____ 5. One way bosses evaluate their employees is by observing them work. Another **approach** that bosses use is face-to-face meetings with employees.

____ 6. Taking college classes allows people to **further** their education. College helps people increase their knowledge about the world.

____ 7. People looking for jobs should **keep in mind** that businesses post jobs in the newspaper and on the Internet.

____ 8. Before applying for a job, you need to make sure you have experience that **is relevant to** the position. Employers want people who have held jobs with similar responsibilities.

____ 9. As a business owner, Carlos needs to have a lot of **initiative**. He must make many important decisions about the way his company works.

____ 10. After you have a job interview, the employer will usually **get in touch with** you by phone or mail to tell you if you got the job or not.

a. someone you know, but who is not a close friend
b. be directly related to the subject or problem being discussed or considered
c. a person you know who may be able to help you or give you advice about something
d. write or speak to someone on the telephone in order to tell them something
e. help something succeed or be achieved
f. likely to develop into a particular type of person or thing in the future
g. a method of doing something or dealing with a problem
h. remember a fact or piece of information, especially because it might be useful to you or might affect you in the future
i. the ability to make decisions and take actions without waiting for someone else to tell you what to do
j. a person, book, or document that supplies you with information

READING 1

How Networking Works

1 "It's not what you know, it's who you know." This old saying, while not entirely accurate, contains an element of truth. When it comes to planning careers and seeking jobs, networking pays off.[1] Networking—the process of taking advantage of relationships with other people for career or professional purposes—can be a key part of occupational[2] success.

2 "Networking is clearly the single most important avenue to successful career planning, career choice, and implementation,[3]" says Jack R. Rayman, Ph.D., director of career services at Penn State University. "Most people who hold really good positions got there through networking."

3 According to career experts, fewer than half of all jobs are advertised. For the others, as well as for many publicized jobs, the secret to success is networking. "Given a choice between two equally qualified candidates, hiring managers will usually prefer a person with whom he or she has had a previous positive experience," says Dr. Janet Scarborough, a career counselor with Bridgeway Career Development in Mercer Island, Washington. "That is why networking is so important—because it

(continued)

[1] **pay off:** offer an advantage or profit as a result of doing something
[2] **occupational:** relating to your job
[3] **implementation:** the act of beginning to make a plan, process, etc., happen

brings you into contact with more **potential** hiring managers."

Making Contacts

4 Just how do you get involved in networking? Actually, it's not that hard. You're probably already part of several networks. As a student, you know teachers, coaches, counselors, and the relatives of other students. Wherever you live, you probably have neighbors. You also have a number of other **acquaintances**; the person who cuts your hair, your doctor and dentist, the small-business owner who lives down the street. Add to that people you know from your own activities, such as religious groups, clubs, or volunteer organizations, and you've just put together your own pool of **contacts**.

5 Taking advantage of these contacts is what networking is all about. When you are looking for a job or otherwise trying to get ahead, you can use these people as **sources** of help or information. In some cases, contacts are employers whom you can speak to directly about possible jobs. In other cases, they may be able to refer you to contacts of their own. Either way, the contacts are worth cultivating.[4] And there is nothing wrong with that **approach**.

6 "The biggest misconception[5] about networking is that it is somehow unfair to take advantage of your personal and/or professional network to **further** your own career," Rayman says. "That's not the case at all." Consider the case of David, a high school sophomore who wanted to earn money to buy a car. One Sunday at the conclusion of church services, he walked up to Dr. Sandway, a local veterinarian,[6] and asked if he ever needed part-time employees. Not only were the two acquainted from attending the same church, but they had also served together as part of a mission team that helped repair homes damaged by a hurricane. Dr. Sandway said he knew David was a good worker, and he would let him know if he needed a new employee. Less than a week later, he called David and offered him a part-time job at his clinic.

7 You can take similar action. First, identify the various people in your life who might serve as useful contacts. Then let them know that you are seeking employment or advice. This might involve making phone calls, writing letters, or approaching contacts in person. In the process, avoid being pushy[7] or demanding. Be both direct and polite. Make statements such as "If you have any job openings, I'd appreciate being considered" or "If you know of any job opportunities, would you mind letting me know?" Make sure your contacts know how to reach you, and be sure to follow up with a thank-you note or call whenever a contact provides any type of help.

8 **Keep in mind** that you don't need to be actively involved in job hunting to network. In fact, students can begin the networking process while still in school. "Perhaps the first thing students should do is establish strong relationships with their teachers," says Rayman. "It's best to focus on those who are most connected in the world of work." Students might also consider the value of working as interns[8] or part-timers.

[4] **cultivate:** make an effort to develop a friendly relationship with someone, especially someone who can help you

[5] **misconception:** an idea that is wrong or untrue, but that people believe because they do not understand it correctly

[6] **veterinarian:** someone who is trained to give medical care and treatment to sick animals

[7] **pushy:** so determined to succeed to get what you want that you behave in an impolite way

[8] **intern:** someone, especially a student, who works for a short time in a particular job in order to gain experience, often for little or no money

"Internships and part-time jobs that **are relevant to** a future career are a better investment than are jobs that might be fun but are not résumé-builders," says Scarborough.

Helpful Traits

9 What are the most important qualities or traits needed to network successfully? According to Rayman, they include confidence, **initiative**, and the ability to interact comfortably with others. Don't be shy about developing new contacts to add to the ones you already have. For example, if you have ideas about career areas you'd like to explore, **get in touch with** adults working in those areas, and ask about the field in question. "Most professionals are flattered to be contacted by young people seeking to enter their profession, and thus are thrilled to interact with them and share insights[9] about their career experience," he says. "Sometimes they are even in a position to offer employment."

10 Whether you're interacting with new contacts or an existing network, keep in mind that you can't have too many friends and acquaintances. The more people you know, the better your chances of networking successfully.

[9] **insight:** a sudden clear understanding of what something is really like

Identifying Main Ideas

Match each paragraph with its main idea.

__b__ paragraph 3

____ paragraph 4

____ paragraph 6

____ paragraph 8

____ paragraph 9

a. People have several networks through the people they already know.
b. Networking improves your chances of getting a job, whether it is publicized or not.
c. Networking successfully requires confidence, initiative, and the ability to interact with others.
d. It is not wrong to take advantage of the contacts you have to help you get a job.
e. People should begin networking when they are still in school.

Identifying Details

These steps are not in correct order. Scan paragraph 7 and number the steps from 1–4.

____ Let your contacts know you are looking for a job.

____ Tell your contacts how to reach you if they know about a job.

____ Identify people in your life that would be useful contacts.

____ Send a thank-you note when a contact helps you.

Making Inferences

Infer what the writer would say is true even though it is not directly stated. Check (✔) each statement the writer would agree with.

____ 1. Networking will often get you a better job.

____ 2. Friends are better contacts than teachers.

____ 3. Many people use their neighbors as business contacts.

____ 4. A number of people don't understand how networking works.

____ 5. It is possible to upset people if you don't network correctly.

Recognizing Time Markers and Sequence Markers

Writers use **time markers** and **sequence markers** when they write about a series of steps that happen in a specific order. Time and sequence markers make the order of the steps clearer to the reader.

To show this time-order sequence, writers use *adverbs*, *prepositional phrases*, and *time clauses*.

EXAMPLE

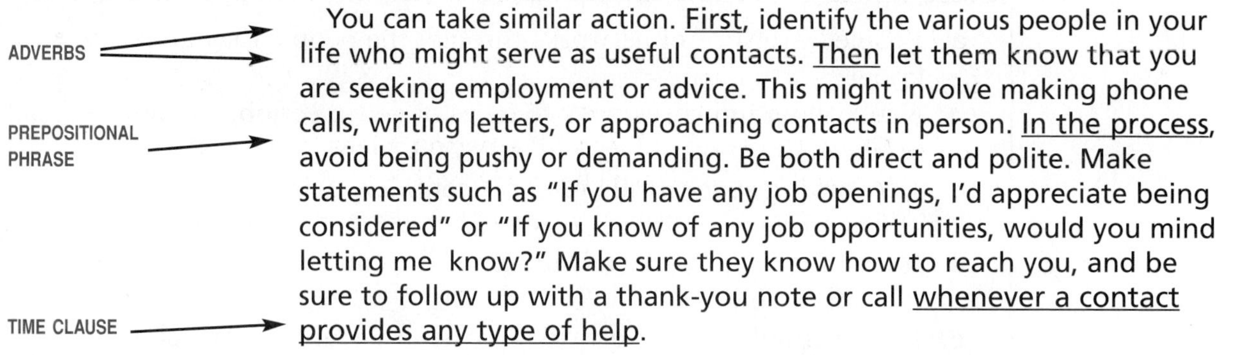

You can take similar action. First, identify the various people in your life who might serve as useful contacts. Then let them know that you are seeking employment or advice. This might involve making phone calls, writing letters, or approaching contacts in person. In the process, avoid being pushy or demanding. Be both direct and polite. Make statements such as "If you have any job openings, I'd appreciate being considered" or "If you know of any job opportunities, would you mind letting me know?" Make sure they know how to reach you, and be sure to follow up with a thank-you note or call whenever a contact provides any type of help.

Practice

Read the paragraph. Circle the time and sequence markers.

Are You Ready to Network?

Here's a quick way to get started building your own network. First, get a stack of index cards (or use your computer). On separate cards, write a heading for each of the different groups of people you know or groups you belong to. Include headings such as *Teachers, Neighbors, Mom's Family, Dad's Family, Youth Groups, Coaches, Volunteer Groups,* and so forth. Next, go back to each card and write down the names of people you know who fit under that heading. Highlight those who seem to offer the most potential as contacts, and add information such as addresses, phone numbers, and e-mail addresses. When you begin looking for a job, use these lists as a starting point. Call, write, or otherwise get in touch with anyone who might be a possible employer or who might refer you to those considering new hires.

VOCABULARY SKILL

Using Idioms with *Get*

An **idiom** is a group of words which has a special meaning that is different from the meaning of each word on its own. Look at the following idioms that use the verb *get* and their meanings.

get in touch with: call or write to someone
get to the point: say the important part of what you want to say
get to know: become familiar with a person, place, system, etc.
get a handle on: start to understand something
get (something) across: successfully communicate an idea to someone

Practice

Complete each sentence with the correct* get *idiom.

1. After studying for three straight hours, Wendy is finally getting *a handle on* the new math concepts her teacher presented in class yesterday.
2. Before looking for a job, you should get ________________ your contacts to see if they know about any possible job opportunities.
3. Business managers interview potential employees so they can get ________________ them better.
4. Good leaders are able to get their ideas ________________ to others in a simple and direct way.
5. It is a good idea to get ________________ quickly when you answer questions at a job interview. Interviewers don't want to waste time on unnecessary details.

FROM READING TO WRITING

Journal
Choose one of your answers and write a journal entry.

Reflecting on the Reading

Discuss the questions in pairs or small groups.

1. Do you think getting a job through networking is fair or unfair? Explain.
2. What kind of contacts do you think are the most helpful in getting a job—friends, teachers, or relatives? Explain.

PRE-READING 2

Discussion

Discuss the questions in pairs or small groups.

1. Is having a well-paid job as important as having a job you love? Explain.
2. If you could start your own business, what kind of business would it be?

Vocabulary

Read the article. Match each boldfaced word with the definition in the box. Write the letter.

The Google™ Success Story

Anyone who uses the Internet on a daily basis is familiar with Google.com™. However, not everyone knows of the story behind it. In 1998, two computer-science majors, Larry Page and Sergei Brin, used their **expertise** (1____) in computers to **come up with** (2____) a new way to organize and search through websites on the Internet. They wanted to **turn** what they had learned in school **into** (3____) something **practical** (4____)—something that everyone could use. With little money, these two student **entrepreneurs** (5____) started their own company. At first, their company was very small. They **operated** (6____) the business out of a small garage and had only a few employees. Three years later, their company had more than 1,000 workers and had become world famous, making over $1 billion a year in profits. What led to such an amazing **accomplishment** (7____)? Having a great knowledge of computers, believing in their product, and being willing to take risks **were vital** (8____) **to** Page's and Brin's success. They represent the true success story, and their company continues to impact the world—one website at a time.

a. designed to be useful, or be suitable for a particular purpose; relating to real situations and events rather than ideas
b. someone who starts a company, arranges business deals, and takes risks in order to make a profit
c. extremely important and necessary for something to succeed or exist
d. special skills or knowledge in a particular subject that you learn by experience or training
e. something successful or impressive that is achieved after a lot of effort and hard work
f. become something different, or make someone or something be different
g. organize and manage a business or activity
h. think of an idea, plan, answer, etc.

READING 2

How to Run a Successful Business

1 Anyone with a marketable idea and the initiative to make it work can start a business. Do you have what it takes? This article will help you find out.

2 Mike Moylan and his brother, Brendan, were only high school students when they took the biggest step of their lives. They launched[1] Eurosport, a catalog business that sells soccer equipment and related products. "We were not the most sophisticated[2] businesspeople in the world, but we understood the game of soccer," says Brendan in *Entrepreneur Magazine*'s "Young Millionaires" by Rieva Lesonsky. "People let us know right away that there was a market for our **expertise**." That was in 1984. Today, the two brothers have renamed their business Sports Endeavors. In 1997, sales exceeded $38 million. By 2005, sales had exceeded $150 million. "We were in the right place at the right time," says Brendan.

Business Sense

3 But it's not just luck that **turns** a good idea **into** a great success. Six-figure CEOs[3]—whether teenagers or adults—are not born with the skills and abilities necessary to mass-market a product or service successfully. Becoming an **entrepreneur**, or businessperson, is a learning process, says Robin Anderson, a business professor and director of the Center for Entrepreneurship at the University of Portland in Oregon. Anderson says businesses motivate students to learn skills that connect them with the real world.

4 Take, for instance, Jennifer Kushell, author of *The Young Entrepreneur's Edge: Using Your Ambition, Independence, and Youth to Launch a Successful Business*. By the age of 19, Jennifer had **operated** four businesses: They involved T-shirts, gift baskets, women's safety seminars,[4] and videotapes of college tours. Hands-on experience taught Jennifer a lot about business, but she wanted to learn more. She started reading entrepreneur-related books and magazines and began attending conferences and seminars. At a conference, she **came up with** her best moneymaking business: The Young Entrepreneurs Network, an organization that supports and educates entrepreneurs, and puts members into contact with other young businesspeople.

What It Takes

5 Most entrepreneurs are not Ivy-League[5] whiz kids[6] like Robert Sundara, who graduated from Stanford and founded a multimillion dollar sporting-goods site, FogDog. Still, it takes a certain kind of person to be an entrepreneur. You must be a

[1] **launch:** start something new, such as an activity, plan, or business

[2] **sophisticated:** having a lot of knowledge and experience in difficult or complicated subjects, and therefore able to understand them well

[3] **CEO:** (Chief Executive Officer) the person with the most authority in a large company (Six-figure CEOs make $100,000 per year or more.)

[4] **seminar:** a class or series of classes for a small group of students, in which they study or talk about a particular subject

[5] **Ivy League:** relating to a group of eight old respected universities in the northeastern U.S, including Harvard, Yale, and Princeton

[6] **whiz kid:** a young person who is very skilled or successful at something

risk-taker, for one thing. You must be creative and enjoy working hard in an area you find fascinating. You also must enjoy the independence and responsibility of being your own boss. "I like having my own hours," says D'Arcy Marlow, 18, who operates a bench-building business. D'Arcy makes benches during spring, summer, and winter breaks at West Texas A&M University.

6 To succeed as an entrepreneur, it also helps to be skilled in a **practical** area. Maybe you like to garden, make crafts, or build furniture. Or perhaps you can fix appliances or bikes or whip up[7] a tasty dessert. For example, brothers Sean, Brenden, and Paddy O'Connell realized they had the skills to teach younger kids the basics of basketball. So the three teens organized the O'Connell Basketball Camp in River Forest, Illinois. They turned a hobby they loved into a business that pays. So did Regina Jackson, 18, of Washington, D.C. She took $50 and talent for crafting beautiful ornaments and opened a jewelry design business. Her long-range goal is to own an international chain of shops.

7 Entrepreneurs also must be hard-working. By the time Katie Beeman, from Duluth, Minnesota, was 18, she had started and operated two successful businesses: a lawn service and a Christmas tree lot. Thanks to this experience and her school **accomplishments**, she won a four-year Young Entrepreneurial Business Scholarship to the University of St. Thomas.

8 It's important for businesspeople to be able to recognize a good idea and act quickly to implement it. Take Claire Meunier. The 17-year-old New Orleans high-schooler made a campus survival pack as a gift for an older brother going off to college. When the idea began attracting attention, Claire recognized its moneymaking potential. So last year she surveyed college kids, tapped[8] family and friends for financial information, and wrote a business plan for her company, Meunier's Commodities. The plan won the Independent Means National Business Plan Competition. Now a freshman at Vanderbilt University, Claire has decided to become a business major.

[7] **whip up:** to quickly make something to eat

Turn Bytes into Bucks

9 A knowledge of computers **is vital to** becoming an entrepreneur, reports *Young Biz*'s "Report on Youth Entrepreneurship." At least 75 percent of the top 100 businesses use computers to perform tasks. And the three highest moneymaking categories are computer-related. Take Rishi Bhat, 15, for example. A 10th grader from Chicago, Rishi co-wrote a computer program, SiegeSoft, which lets people surf the Internet anonymously.[9] He then set up a website to market copies of the program. Within a few months, Rishi sold the program for $1.6 million.

Just Do It!

10 Joshua Fagan, from Camarillo, California, recently won a $12,000 college scholarship from the National Association for the Self-Employed for his business, Cute Stuff Artworks, which sells creative art for children's rooms. "Entrepreneurs succeed because they don't just wish things would happen. They make them happen," Joshua, 15, said in a recent interview.

[8] **tap:** make as much use as possible of the ideas, experience, knowledge, etc. that a group of people has

[9] **anonymously:** without giving your name

Identifying Main Ideas

Match the people with the main idea they illustrate in the reading.

____ 1. D'Arcy Mallow

____ 2. Sean, Brenden, and Paddy O'Connell

____ 3. Katie Beeman

____ 4. Claire Meunier

____ 5. Rishi Bhat

a. Entrepreneurs recognize a good idea and implement it quickly.
b. Entrepreneurs have a knowledge of computers.
c. Entrepreneurs are skilled in a practical area.
d. Entrepreneurs enjoy the independence and responsibility of being their own boss.
e. Entrepreneurs are hard-working.

Identifying Details

Match the people with the company or product they started.

____ 1. Mike and Brendan Moylan

____ 2. Jennifer Kushell

____ 3. Robert Sundara

____ 4. Rishi Bhat

____ 5. Joshua Fagan

a. SiegeSoft
b. Eurosport/Sports Endeavors
c. The Young Entrepreneurs Network
d. FogDog
e. Cute Stuff Artworks

Making Inferences

Infer what the writer would say is true even though it is not directly stated. Check (✓) the statements the writer would agree with.

____ 1. Not everyone has the skills necessary to run his or her own successful business.

____ 2. It's easier to start your own business if you have a lot of money.

____ 3. Not knowing how to use computers makes it harder to succeed in business.

____ 4. Age does not determine how successful a person can become.

____ 5. Most new businesses today are started on the Internet.

FROM READING TO WRITING

> ***Vocabulary***
> For more practice with vocabulary, go to pages 176–177.

Reflecting on the Reading

Discuss the questions in pairs or small groups.

1. Reading 2 illustrated the benefits of risk-taking. Discuss one "good risk" you have taken in your own life.
2. Who is the most successful person you know? How did he or she become successful?

WRITING

> ***Journal***
> Choose one of your answers and write a journal entry.

The Process Essay

Process essays discuss a series of steps in chronological (time) order. They can explain how to do or accomplish a task. Reading 1 gave steps on how to network with people to get a job. Reading 2 explained how young entrepreneurs can start and run their own business. Many process essays in college focus on technical or complex procedures. In an economics course, a process essay could explain how to buy and sell stocks. A government course might require you to explain how a country elects its politicians.

Read the model essay. What three steps does the essay discuss?

MODEL

Job Interviewing 101

Author Mark Twain once said that "work is a necessary evil to be avoided." Unfortunately, most people cannot avoid work. Consequently, they also cannot avoid job interviews. Employers require interviews because they want to know if you will be a good fit for the company. Knowing how to interview is vital to getting the job you want. By following three simple steps, you can succeed at a job interview and get the job you want.

First of all, in order to succeed at a job interview, you need to be well prepared. Before your interview, you should find out as much information about

(continued)

your potential employer as possible. The Internet can be a great source of information about a business. Look on the Internet to see what the company is involved in and how it operates. You also need to practice what you are going to say when the interviewer asks you about your experience and accomplishments. Come up with possible questions he or she might ask, and practice interviewing with a friend or family member until you know exactly what you are going to say. Be sure that the information you will provide about yourself is directly relevant to the job.

On the day of the interview, you need to help yourself relax. Being nervous at a job interview can cause things to go terribly wrong. Luckily, there are ways to help yourself stay calm before an interview. You can listen to calming music, or close your eyes and visualize a peaceful image, such as a beach at sunset. Don't let any bad thoughts come into your mind. Stay focused, and take deep breaths. Controlling your breathing is one of the best ways to keep your body relaxed.

Finally, at the interview it is important to be polite. Make sure you arrive to the interview on time. Being late to an interview will not only make you nervous, but it will also make the interviewer wonder whether you might be late to work in the future. Not arriving on time is disrespectful, and most employers won't hire you if you don't follow this simple rule. It is also impolite to talk when interviewers are talking. Tell them everything you want to say, but never interrupt them, and always listen closely when they are talking.

In summary, you will do well at a job interview if you follow this step-by-step approach. Job interviews are a necessary evil, and they can be very intimidating. However, you will thank yourself if you take this advice. It is helpful to keep in mind that a good job interview will usually get you the job you desire.

WRITING SKILL

Organizing the Process Essay

These steps will help you organize your process essay.

Introduction

- Introduce the process.
- Provide background information on who goes through this process, why people go through it, and/or when this process occurs.
- Write a thesis statement.

Thesis Statement The thesis statement for a process essay should state the topic and show that the essay will give a series of steps.

EXAMPLE

By following three simple steps, you can succeed at a job interview and get the job you want.

Body Divide the process into three or four major steps. Write one body paragraph for each step, and put them in chronological order. Use time and sequence markers in your topic sentences to show the order of the steps (see p. 26).

EXAMPLES

First of all, in order to succeed at a job interview, you need to be well prepared.

On the day of the interview, you need to help yourself relax.

Finally, at the interview it is important to be polite.

Conclusion Write a restated thesis. Offer final thoughts on what the end result(s) of the process will be and why following the steps correctly is important.

EXAMPLE

In summary, you will do well at a job interview if you follow this step-by-step approach.

Practice

Discuss the topics below in pairs or small groups. List three steps for each process.

1. How to stay safe when driving
   a. ______________________________
   b. ______________________________
   c. ______________________________
2. How to prepare for a test
   a. ______________________________
   b. ______________________________
   c. ______________________________
3. How to live on a small budget
   a. ______________________________
   b. ______________________________
   c. ______________________________

WRITING SKILL

Writing an Effective Introduction

The introduction of an essay has three elements: the lead, the background information, and the thesis statement.

Look at these three elements in the introduction from the model essay.

LEAD / BACKGROUND INFORMATION / THESIS STATEMENT

Author Mark Twain once said that "work is a necessary evil to be avoided." Unfortunately, most people cannot avoid work. Consequently, they also cannot avoid job interviews. Employers require interviews because they want to know if you will be a good fit for the company, and knowing how to interview is vital to getting the job you want. By following three simple steps, you can succeed at a job interview and get the job you want.

The **lead** comes at the beginning of the introduction. The lead introduces the topic of the essay in two or three sentences. It needs to capture the readers' attention and make them want to continue reading. The most common leads writers use are:

- **asking a question**

  EXAMPLE

  Why are job interviews so important?

- **using a famous quote or proverb**

  EXAMPLE

  Author Mark Twain once said that "work is a necessary evil to be avoided."

- **giving statistics or interesting facts**

  EXAMPLE

  Every day millions of people go searching for a job.

- **offering an interesting observation or opinion**

  EXAMPLE

  Unfortunately, most people cannot avoid work. Consequently, they also cannot avoid job interviews.

- **telling a short story (an anecdote)**

  EXAMPLE

  I had been preparing all week, and the day had finally arrived. I was very nervous at my first job interview. I didn't know what to expect, but I did my best. Twenty-four hours later, I heard those magical words, "Congratulations. You got the job."

Background information is important information about the topic that readers need to know in order to understand the rest of the essay.

The thesis statement is usually the last sentence of the introduction. It states the main idea of the essay.

Practice

Read this introduction and follow the instructions below.

It is safe to say that students are not the richest people in the world. In fact, some studies have shown that most college seniors will have more than $19,000 of debt when they graduate. Struggling students need to understand how to live on a budget, which means knowing how much money they have and not spending any more than they have. For students, living on a budget involves following a three-step process.

1. This introduction uses two types of leads. What are they?
2. Underline the sentence that gives background information about the topic.
3. Double underline the thesis statement.

WRITING ASSIGNMENT

Write a process essay. Follow the steps.

STEP 1 Get ideas.

A. Choose a topic for your essay. Check (✔) it.

❑ **Topic 1:** Steps you will take to achieve a specific career goal

❑ **Topic 2:** How to handle studying and working at the same time

❑ **Topic 3:** How people can find the career that is right for them

B. Make a list of all the steps you will discuss. Combine steps that are closely related to each other. Choose the three or four most important steps to use in your essay.

STEP 2 Organize your ideas.

Make an outline for your essay.

STEP 3 Write a rough draft.

Write your essay. Use your outline from Step 2 to help you. Include vocabulary from the unit where possible.

STEP 4 Revise your rough draft.

Read your essay. Use the Writing Checklist to look for mistakes. Work alone or in pairs.

Writing Checklist

- ❑ Does your process essay introduction:
  - have an interesting lead?
  - give background information about the process?
  - have a clear thesis statement that states the topic and indicates the essay will give a series of steps?
- ❑ Do your body paragraphs present the steps in chronological order?
- ❑ Does your conclusion have a restated thesis?
- ❑ Did you include time and sequence markers appropriately in your essay?

STEP 5 Edit your writing.

A. Edit your essay. Use the correction symbols chart on page 173. Correct any mistakes in capitalization, punctuation, spelling, verb-tense, and the use of gerunds as subjects and gerunds (*-ing* forms) as objects.

When a verb is used as a subject or object, it is changed to a gerund (*-ing*):

EXAMPLES

GERUND: *Controlling*

~~Control~~ your breathing will help you stay relaxed.

GERUND: *making*

Don't be afraid of ~~make~~ mistakes when you start a new job.

B. Work in pairs. Exchange essays and check each other's work.

STEP 6 Write a final copy.

Correct your mistakes. Copy your final essay and give it to your instructor.

UNIT

3

The Environment

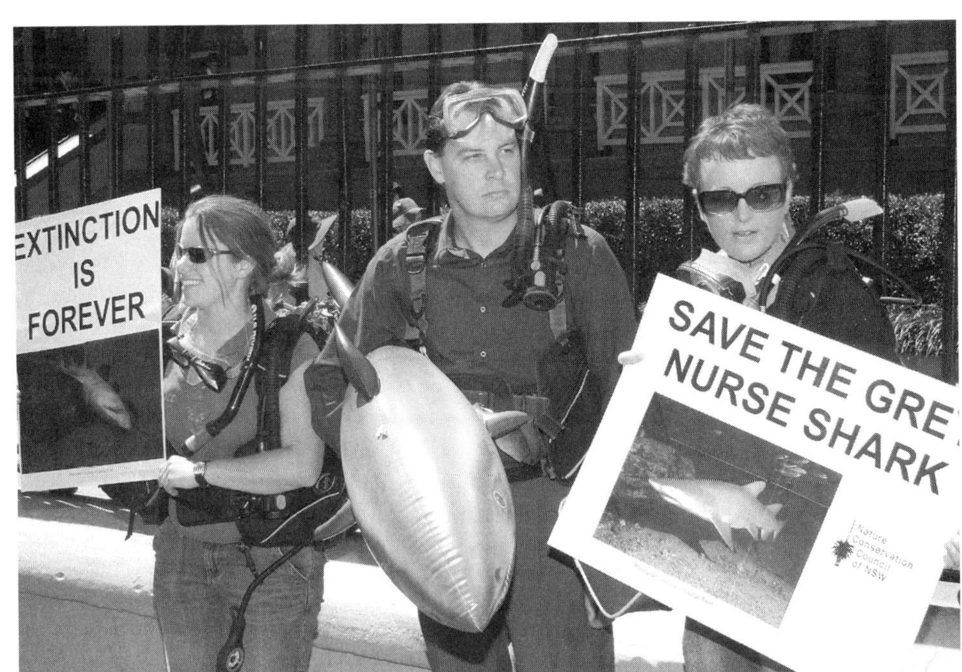

In this unit you will:

- read articles about cell-phone recycling and underground aquifers
- learn to recognize coherence markers
- organize and write a problem-solution essay
- learn to write an effective conclusion

PRE-READING 1

Discussion

Discuss the questions in pairs or small groups.

1. Look at the picture. What are these people protesting against?
2. Electronic waste, or e-waste, refers to electrical devices that people throw away. What kinds of devices cause e-waste?
3. What do you think is the most serious environmental problem in the world today? Explain.

Vocabulary

Read the boldfaced words and their definitions. Then complete the paragraph with the correct words. Change the form of words as needed.

contribute to: help make something happen
demand: the need or desire for particular goods or services
diminish: become smaller, less, or less important, or make something do this
dramatic: surprising and often impressive
highlight: put importance on; draw attention to
ideal: the most appropriate for someone or for a specific job
impact: the effect or influence that an event or situation has on someone or something
objective: something to be achieved
point out: tell someone something that they do not already know or have not thought about

Recycling

Recycling has two main (1) ______________: to reduce the amount of trash people make and to keep our environment healthy. Recycling can have a(n) (2) ______________ effect on the environment. For example, environmental groups (3) ______________ that recycling just one ton (2,000 lbs.) of paper saves 17 trees from being cut down. Recycling also has a positive (4) ______________ on energy conservation. As the global population rises, the world's (5) ______________ for energy also increases. However, recycling can (6) ______________ the amount of energy people use. For instance, recycling glass requires 40 percent less energy than making new glass. These two facts (7) ______________ just how beneficial recycling can be. It (8) ______________ the survival of plants and animals, and it also helps to save the earth's resources. Recycling programs are (9) ______________ for any community that is trying to save energy and reduce its waste.

READING 1

Can Cell-Phone Recycling Help African Gorillas?

By Stefan Lorgren

1 Recycle your cell phone, save the gorillas. It may not be as simple as that, but a recycling program to collect old cell phones at the San Diego Zoo and other American zoos is **highlighting** the little-known connection between cell-phone use and the survival of African gorillas.

2 Conservationists[1] **point out** that recycling cell phones protects landfills[2] from the many hazardous chemicals in the phones, including antimony, arsenic, copper, cadmium, lead, and zinc. But cell phones also include coltan, a mineral extracted in the deep forests of the Congo in central Africa. These forests are home to the world's endangered[3] lowland gorillas.

3 Because of the worldwide cell-phone boom, the Congo's out-of-control coltan mining business has in recent years led to a **dramatic** reduction of animal habitat. This industry has also led to rampant[4] slaughter of great apes for the illegal bush-meat trade (the hunting of wild animals for food). "Most people don't know that there's a connection between this metal in their cell phones and the well-being of wildlife in the area where it's mined," said Karen Killmar, the associate curator of mammals at the San Diego Zoo. "Recycling old cell phones is a way for people to do something very simple that could reduce the need for additional coltan . . . and help protect the gorillas," she said.

Reselling Phones

4 There are more than 150 million cell-phone users in the United States alone. Because technology is changing so rapidly, the average lifespan of a cell phone is 14 months. There may already be 500 million unused cell phones in the United States, with as many as 100 million added each year.

5 The San Diego Zoo is among 46 zoos with a cell-phone recycling program. The program is run by Eco-Cell, which is based in Louisville, Kentucky. Eco-Cell collected 21,000 phones last year and hopes to triple that figure this year. The phones are sold in bulk to a handful of refurbishing[5] companies. These companies then resell the phones in developing markets, such as Africa and Latin America.

6 Eco-Cell started in 2002 but began concentrating on zoos in 2005. The money it makes from selling the phones goes to supporting various conservation groups, primarily zoos. "It just made business logic to focus on zoos, since 130 million-plus people went to North American zoos last year," said Eco-Cell president, Eric Ronay. "We set up a

(continued)

[1] **conservationist:** someone who works to protect animals, plants, etc.

[2] **landfill:** a place where waste is buried under the ground

[3] **endangered:** in danger of being killed or destroyed, or of not existing anymore

[4] **rampant:** if something is rampant, it is bad, happens often in many different places, and is difficult to control

[5] **refurbish:** thoroughly repair and improve something

collection point at the front gate of those zoos and invited the public to bring in their old cell phones." Ronay said learning about the devastating **impact** of coltan mining on African gorillas "really made light bulbs go off for us."

Illegal Miners

7 Columbite-tantalite—*coltan* for short—is a metallic ore that, when refined,[6] becomes metallic tantalum. Tantalum is heat-resistant and can hold a high electrical charge. These properties are **ideal** for making capacitors, which collect and store energy in electronic devices such as cell phones. Eighty percent of the world's known coltan supply is in the Congo. There, it is mined by groups of men who dig basins in streams, scraping away dirt to get to the muddy coltan underneath.

8 The cell-phone boom in the last decade drew more than 10,000 illegal miners into protected parks in central Africa. "The mining itself certainly destroys habitat, so human activity at the very least disturbs the animals there. But more of what happens is that the animals are hunted and killed," said Killmar, the San Diego Zoo curator. "The impact is nothing but negative." Conflict, illegal mining, and the growing bush-meat trade **have all contributed to** a 70 percent population decline of the eastern lowland gorilla, according to some estimates.

E-Waste

9 Sharon Dewar, a spokesperson for the San Diego Zoo, says the **objective** of the recycling program is conservation education. "Many people have cell phones at home in a drawer that are old, and they don't know what to do with them," she said. "These phones contain toxic[7] elements. What we're saying is, please don't throw your cell phone into a landfill." "If a cell phone can be refurbished, that might also help **diminish** the **demand** for coltan mining. This could in fact help gorillas and other animals in their habitat," she said.

[6] **refined:** a substance that is refined has been made pure by an industrial process

[7] **toxic:** poisonous, or containing poison

Identifying Main Ideas

Match the sentence parts below with those in the box. Then circle the number of the sentence that states the main idea of the reading.

__c__ 1. Zoos help collect used cell phones because . . .

__d__ 2. Recycling cell phones will . . .

__a__ 3. Many people are unaware that . . .

__b__ 4. Illegal coltan mining can cause . . .

__e__ 5. Coltan is used in cell phones because . . .

a. many gorillas are dying because of the boom in cell-phone use.
b. the destruction of animal habitats and the killing of gorillas and other animals.
c. they want to educate people about the connection between cell-phone use and the decline in gorilla populations.
d. reduce hazardous chemicals in landfills and help protect gorilla populations in the Congo.
e. it can hold a high electrical charge.

Identifying Details

Mark the statements* T *(true) or* F *(false). Correct the false statements.

____ 1. The average person will keep the same cell phone for about two years.

____ 2. The cell phones Eco-Cell collects are sold in Africa and Latin America.

____ 3. All of the world's coltan comes from the Congo.

____ 4. The number of eastern lowland gorillas has declined by 70 percent.

____ 5. Many people don't throw away their old cell phones.

Making Inferences

The answers to the questions are not stated directly in the reading. Discuss in pairs or small groups what the writer would think is true.

1. In what way are the eastern lowland gorillas of the Congo victims?
2. Why do people keep cell phones for only 14 months on average?
3. Why are used cell phones often sold in developing countries?

READING SKILL

Recognizing Coherence Markers

Coherence in writing means the ideas between sentences flow smoothly from one to another. Writers use **coherence markers** to help readers identify connections between ideas. Two common coherence markers writers use to repeat ideas are *this* + noun and *these* + noun.

EXAMPLES

But cell phones also include coltan, a mineral extracted in the deep forests of the Congo in central Africa. These forests are home to the world's endangered lowland gorillas.

People are mining for coltan in the deep forests of the Congo. This situation has endangered the survival of eastern lowland gorillas.

In the first example, *these forests* refers back to the deep forests of the Congo in central Africa. In the second example, *This situation* refers to coltan mining in the deep forests of the Congo.

Here is a list of general words writers use with the coherence markers *this* and *these*.

SINGULAR NOUNS	PLURAL NOUNS
this situation	these circumstances
this problem	these conditions
this behavior	these actions
this idea	these attitudes
this view	these beliefs

Practice

A. Look at these excerpts from Reading 1. Circle the coherence markers and underline the idea they refer to in the previous sentence.

1. "Many people have cell phones at home in a drawer that are old, and they don't know what to do with them," she said. "These phones contain toxic elements."

2. The phones are sold in bulk to a handful of refurbishing companies. These companies then resell the phones in developing markets, such as Africa and Latin America.

3. Because of the worldwide cell-phone boom, the Congo's out-of-control coltan mining business has in recent years led to a dramatic reduction of animal habitat. This industry has also caused the rampant slaughter of great apes for the illegal bush-meat trade.
4. Tantalum is heat-resistant and can hold a high electrical charge. These properties are ideal for making capacitors, which collect and store energy in electronic devices such as cell phones.

B. ***Use one of the general nouns in the box to continue the idea from the first sentence.***

actions	~~behavior~~	circumstances	problem	view

1. Some people throw their trash on the street instead of in a trash can. This ___*behavior*___ causes city streets to become polluted.
2. Everyone can help the environment by recycling and by trying to use less energy. Both of these ___actions___ would benefit the health of the planet.
3. Many people believe the environment is everyone's responsibility. This ___view___ is commonly held by people who work closely with nature.
4. Every day, people throw away items that could be recycled. This ___problem___ could be fixed if more people knew about the benefits of recycling.
5. Some countries don't have the technology available to recycle their trash, and some don't have enough money to buy the technology. These ___circumstances___ have made it difficult for them to start recycling programs.

Using a Dictionary

Dictionaries list multiple definitions for words. When you find an unknown word while reading, it is important to choose the definition that fits the **context** of the sentence. The meaning of the word needs to match the meaning of the sentence.

Look at the following definitions of the verb *highlight*:

> **highlight** (v.) 1. make something easy to notice so that people pay attention to it: *Your résumé should highlight your skills and achievements.* 2. mark written words with a special colored pen, or in a different color on a computer, so that you can see them easily: *Highlight the desired file using the arrow keys.* 3. make some parts of your hair a lighter color than the rest

These sentences use the word *highlight,* but the context of each requires a different definition of the word. The context is underlined.

1: The president highlighted the company's strengths in his speech.

2: It is helpful to highlight unknown words as you read.

3: Jan recently highlighted the hair around her face.

Practice

Read the boldfaced words and their definitions. Write the number of the definition that is used in each of the sentences that follow.

1. **contribute** (v.) 1. to give money, help, ideas, etc. to something that a lot of other people are also involved in: *Volunteers contribute about 16,000 hours of work each year to the city.* 2. **contribute to sth** to help make something happen: *Yellow fever contributed to Mudd's early death at age 19.* 3. to write articles, stories, poems, etc. for a newspaper or magazine: *Several hundred people contributed articles, photographs, and cartoons.*

2 a. The growing number of cars in the world has contributed to an increase in pollution.

1 b. People contribute millions of dollars every year to organizations that protect the environment.

2. **ideal** (adj.) 1. something that is ideal is the most appropriate for someone or for a specific job: *My new office is in an ideal location.* 2. the best that something could possibly be: *I realize this isn't an ideal situation.* 3. [only before a noun] an ideal world, job, system, etc. is one that you imagine to be perfect, but that is not likely to exist: *In an ideal world, no one would ever get sick.*

3 a. In an ideal work environment, every employee would be treated fairly.

1 b. Working part-time is ideal for Robert because he is also a part-time student.

3. **demand** (n.) 1. the need or desire that people have for particular goods or services: *There isn't much demand for leaded gasoline anymore.* 2. a strong request for something that shows you believe you have the right to get what you ask for: *Administrators finally bowed to demands that the university be renamed.* 3. something difficult, annoying, or tiring that you need to do or a skill you need to have: *Some working parents worry about the conflicting demands of home and job.*

3 a. It's sometimes difficult for people to deal with the demands of working and studying at the same time.

1 b. Some scientists fear that there won't be enough oil in the future to meet global demand.

FROM READING TO WRITING

Journal
Choose one of your answers and write a journal entry.

Reflecting on the Reading

Discuss the questions in pairs or small groups.

1. Do you think the article on cell phones and gorillas will make you recycle your own cell phone in the future? Explain.
2. What other technological devices do you think people should recycle? Explain.
3. Should all communities have recycling programs? If your community (or another community) does not have one, do you think it might start one? Why or why not?

PRE-READING 2

Discussion

Discuss the questions in pairs or small groups.

1. In addition to recycling cell phones, what are other ways people can help the environment?
2. Do you think it is important for people to limit the amount of water they use? Why or why not?

Vocabulary

Read the article. Match each boldfaced word or phrase with the definition in the box. Write the letter.

Water **scarcity** (1___) is a major problem in dry climates. Deserts, for example, receive less than 10 inches (25 cm) of rain per year. The amount of drinkable water in the world is **finite** (2___)—there is not an endless amount. In deserts, there is not enough water to **sustain** (3___) the people who live there.

Today, scientists are looking for ways to **exploit** (4___) the little rainwater deserts receive. They want to use as much of it as possible for human **consumption** (5___). For example, people can collect the water that **accumulates** (6___) on rooftops and use it for drinking water.

Most people in the world drink water that comes from rivers and lakes. Today, however, some towns in India use rainwater as an **alternative** (7___) source of drinking water. Having another option is very important to the people of India because there is not enough water for everyone. Many scientists are excited about **the prospect of** (8___) reusing rainwater in other parts of the world in the future. They think it could help other countries that don't have enough water for their people.

a. having an end or limit
b. able to be used instead of something else; another
c. support
d. a situation in which there is not enough of something
e. the possibility that something will happen in the future
f. gradually increase in number or amount until there is a large quantity in one place
g. the act of eating or drinking, or the amount of food or drink that is eaten or drunk
h. use something such as materials or skills effectively or completely in order to gain an advantage or profit

READING 2

The Water Beneath Our Feet

1 The Sahara desert in northern Africa is one of the driest spots on earth. It averages only 10 inches of rainfall annually. Due to these harsh conditions, it is also one of the most uninhabitable[1] places in the entire world. In the early 1990s, however, views about the Sahara changed dramatically when scientists made a surprising discovery. They found an immense river hiding deep beneath the sand. UNESCO[2] estimates this underground river contains about 120,000 cubic kilometers of fresh water. Today Libya mines the aquifer[3] to deliver fresh water to its citizens. Scientists recognize the great value of this and other underground aquifers. In fact, many see them as a solution to one of the biggest environmental crises facing the world—global water **scarcity**.

2 "Of all the social and natural crises we humans face, the water crisis is the one that lies at the heart of[4] our survival and that of our planet Earth," says UNESCO Director-General Koichiro Matsuura. Today, there simply isn't enough water for everyone. The amount of fresh water on the planet is **finite**. Less than one percent of it is accessible to humans via rivers and lakes. On top of this, water use has increased sixfold in the last one hundred years. With the global population expected to exceed 9 billion in 2050, scientists believe we must find **alternative** sources to meet future demands.

3 Underground aquifers, such as the Nubian Sandstone Aquifer, just might be the solution scientists have been searching for. These aquifers include immense rivers and lakes a half mile or more below the earth's surface. They can range from thousands to

(continued)

[1] **uninhabitable:** a place that is impossible to live in
[2] **UNESCO:** United Nations Educational, Scientific and Cultural Organization
[3] **aquifer:** a layer of stone or earth under the surface of the ground that contains water

[4] **lie at the heart of something:** be the most important part of something

millions of years old. According to UNESCO, some aquifers are fossil aquifers. They contain trapped water that can only be used once. Others can be used and reused as rainwater **accumulates** below the surface over time.

4 Scientists are extremely excited about **the prospect of** harvesting water from these deep aquifers. UNESCO reports that scientists are attempting to create the first global map of the earth's underground aquifers. By 2003, they had already identified 20 aquifers below Africa alone. Others are located under the Middle East, China, India, and Central and South America. Some scientists speculate[5] that these aquifers could hold enough water to **sustain** billions of people for hundreds of years to come.

5 The Nubian Sandstone Aquifer System illustrates the benefits of using underground aquifers. The system delivers roughly 500,000 cubic meters of water to Libya every day using a complex system of pipes that bring the water to the surface. However, this aquifer also travels below three other countries, which could eventually lead to political problems as well.

6 Some experts predict that countries will begin to race one another in an effort to **exploit** as much water as possible before their neighbors do. According to the UN, disagreements over who owns the underground water could lead to serious conflict between nations. Disagreements over aquifer rights have already occurred in parts of the Middle East. Another potential source of conflict is the Guarani aquifer, which travels underneath Argentina, Brazil, Paraguay, and Uruguay.

7 The UN points out that mining for water could also cause environmental problems. Underground aquifers offer much cleaner water than surface sources because they are more protected. However, they are still very fragile. According to the UN, cleaning an aquifer after it has been polluted is almost impossible. Mining projects must therefore reduce pollution risks so these aquifers are not lost forever.

8 With global water **consumption** increasing rapidly, finding alternative water sources is crucial in this day and age. If we manage them correctly, underground aquifers could be one of the most vital solutions to global water scarcity. In fact, mining our underground lakes and rivers for fresh water has the potential to sustain millions, and even billions, of people around the globe.

[5] **speculate:** think or talk about the possible causes or effects of something without knowing all the facts or details

Identifying Main Ideas

Read the questions. Circle the letter of the best answer.

1. What is the main idea of the reading?
   - **a.** Increased population and pollution have lessened the amount of fresh water on Earth.
   - **b.** The Nubian Sandstone Aquifer is located under four different countries, but it is mined by Libya.

c. Underground aquifers could significantly help solve the problem of global water scarcity.

d. Underground aquifers contain cleaner water than rivers and lakes on the Earth's surface.

2. What is the main idea of paragraph 2?

   a. Almost all of the fresh water that people use comes from lakes and rivers.

   b. By 2050, the global population is expected to exceed 9 billion people.

   c. There isn't enough water on Earth to support present and future demands.

   d. People demand six times more water than they did one hundred years ago.

3. What is the main idea of paragraph 5?

   a. Libya gets 500,000 cubic meters of water from aquifers every day.

   b. The Nubian Sandstone Aquifer System travels under four countries.

   c. Many lakes and rivers are located on borders between countries.

   d. Underground aquifers have benefits, but they also have some risks.

4. What is the main idea of paragraph 6?

   a. International conflict can occur because aquifers travel under many different countries.

   b. There are underground aquifers in South America and the Middle East.

   c. Neighboring countries have not yet fought against one another for water.

   d. The Guarani aquifer travels under Argentina, Brazil, Paraguay, and Uruguay.

Identifying Details

Mark the statements* T *(true) or* F *(false).

__F__ 1. Most of the world's fresh water comes from rivers and lakes.

__T__ 2. Underground aquifers can be found in many parts of the world.

__F__ 3. Scientists have discovered almost all of the planet's underground aquifers. Some

__T__ 4. The Guarani aquifer is located in South America.

__F__ 5. It is impossible to pollute underground aquifers because they are well-protected.

Making Inferences

What meaning can be inferred from these sentences from the reading? Circle the letter of the best answer.

1. Scientists are extremely excited about the prospect of harvesting water from these deep aquifers.
   a. Scientists don't know how to harvest underground water yet.
   b. Mining underground aquifers is a relatively new procedure.
   c. There are not many aquifers deep below the earth's surface.
2. UNESCO reports that scientists are attempting to create the first global map of the earth's hidden aquifers.
   a. Scientists don't think aquifers will solve global water scarcity.
   b. Scientists don't know how to find new underground aquifers.
   c. Scientists are not sure how many aquifers exist underground.
3. According to the UN, disagreements over who owns the underground water could lead to serious conflict between nations.
   a. Disagreements over shared aquifers could result in war.
   b. Many people believe aquifers shouldn't belong to anyone.
   c. Most underground aquifers are already owned by countries.

FROM READING TO WRITING

Journal
Choose one of your answers and write a journal entry.

Reflecting on the Reading

Discuss the questions in pairs or small groups.

1. After reading the article on the global water crisis, do you think you will reduce the amount of water you use? Why or why not?
2. How can people reduce the amount of water they use on a daily basis? Explain.
3. Do you believe richer countries should help poorer countries that do not have enough clean water for their people? Explain.

WRITING

Vocabulary
For more practice with vocabulary, go to pages 178–179.

The Problem-Solution Essay

A problem-solution essay analyzes the aspects of a problematic situation and offers possible solutions for that situation. Reading 1 discussed how the cell-phone industry has caused problems for African gorillas, and explained how recycling can help improve this situation. Likewise,

Reading 2 presented the problem of global water scarcity, and suggested how underground aquifers could help solve this problem. Problem-solution essays are used in many college courses. Sociology students can write about social problems such as crime or inequality; in a business course, you might offer ways to maximize profits; and essays for a biology course could explore the problem of an endangered species.

Read the model essay. What problem does the essay discuss? What solutions does it offer?

MODEL

Rain Forests: Our Last Good-bye?

At one time, rain forests covered 14 percent of the earth's surface. Today, they cover less than 6 percent, and some experts predict that in 40 years, they may no longer exist. People are exploiting the world's rain forests, from the Amazon rain forest of South America to those in Africa and Southeast Asia. Rain forest deforestation has major consequences on the planet, but the problem can be solved if people take the right steps.

Rain forest deforestation has a dramatic effect on plants, animals, and the environment. Many of today's medicines are made from rain forest plants, but there are still thousands to discover. If we destroy them before we discover them, we might also destroy a possible cure for cancer or AIDS. The rain forests also sustain a variety of animal life. Deforestation forces these animals to move to new locations, and many die because they can't find a new home. Deforestation also has an impact on the health of the planet. Fewer trees on the earth mean that more carbon dioxide accumulates in the atmosphere. This situation can result in global warming.

These problems are significant, but there are ways solve them. Many of the countries with rain forests do not have enough money to control deforestation. Richer countries could offer financial aid to these countries to help them stop illegal deforestation. Average citizens could also help financially by contributing money to rain forest charities. However, money will not end destruction indefinitely. The ideal way to solve this problem is to educate all people about the consequences of rain forest destruction. People who cut down the rain forests need to understand that they are hurting the environment. Furthermore, everyone around the world must know about the connection between deforestation and the future health of the planet. If more people know about it, more people will take action to try and stop it.

(continued)

In conclusion, it is possible to solve the crisis of the rain forests. To meet this objective, it is essential that people work together. If we all ignore the problem, we will risk losing the rain forests forever. We must take action now. The earth, our children, and our grandchildren are depending on it.

Organizing the Problem-Solution Essay

The **thesis statement** for a problem-solution essay should identify the main problem (the topic), and indicate that the essay will provide solutions for it.

EXAMPLE

Global warming creates many problems for the environment, but it could be solved if people made simple changes in the way they live.

In the **first body paragraph**, list the specific problems the main problem causes.

- 1st specific problem
- 2nd specific problem
- 3rd specific problem

In the **second body paragraph**, list solutions to the problems in the same sequence.

- 1st solution
- 2nd solution
- 3rd solution

Begin the **conclusion** with a **restated thesis**. Then predict what will happen if the problem is not fixed.

Practice

Read the model essay again. Complete the outline with the information.

I. Introduction

A. Lead: At one time... They may no longer exist.

B. Background information: *People are exploiting the world's rain forests, from the Amazon rain forest of South America to those in Africa and Southeast Asia.*

C. Thesis statement: Rain forest deforestation has major consequences on the planet, but the problem can be solved if people take the right steps.

II. Body

A. Topic sentence: __________

1. *It destroys undiscovered plants.*
2. __________
3. __________

B. Topic sentence: __________

1. *Richer countries could offer financial aid to countries with rain forests to help stop illegal deforestation.*
2. __________
3. __________

III. Conclusion

A. Restated thesis: __________

B. Prediction: *If we all ignore the problem, we will risk losing the rain forests forever.*

Writing the Conclusion

The conclusion finishes the essay and gives the writer's final ideas about the topic. The conclusion has two main elements: the **restated thesis** and **final thoughts**.

- **The restated thesis is usually the first sentence of the conclusion**. It might begin with a conclusion connector, such as *In conclusion*, *In summary*, *In all*, *To conclude*, or *To summarize*. It repeats the same idea in the thesis statement but in different words.

EXAMPLE

Thesis: Rain forest deforestation has major consequences on the planet, but the problem can be solved if people take the right steps.

Restated thesis: In conclusion, it is possible to solve the crisis of the rain forests.

- **Final thoughts should not introduce any new topics**. They might reflect on what the essay has already said or offer an idea or suggestion to think about in the future.

EXAMPLES

It is essential that people work together to stop the destruction of rain forests.

If we all ignore the problem, we will risk losing the rain forests forever. We must take action now. The earth, our children, and our grandchildren are depending on it.

Practice

Read this conclusion from an essay on endangered animals. Then answer the questions.

In all, there is more than one way to help save endangered animals. The fact is that today too many animals are losing their lives. We have caused them to be endangered, but we also have the power to save them. It is our responsibility to take control of the situation. It may be difficult, but it will definitely be worth the effort.

1. What is the restated thesis? Underline it.
2. Which sentence reflects on what the essay has already said?
3. Which sentences offer ideas to think about in the future?

WRITING ASSIGNMENT

Write a problem-solution essay. Follow the steps.

STEP 1 **Get ideas.**

A. Choose a topic for your essay. Check (✔) it.

❑ **Topic 1:** In many cities, there are too many cars on the road. What consequences does that have on the environment? What can people do to solve the problem?

❑ **Topic 2:** The amount of garbage, or trash, people make is increasing. What negative effects does this have on the environment? How can this problem be solved?

❑ **Topic 3:** What is one environmental problem in your community? Explain the problem and suggest possible solutions.

B. Make a list of problems and solutions for your topic.

Problems	Solutions

STEP 2 **Organize your ideas.**

Make an outline for a four-paragraph essay on your topic. Choose ideas from Step 1.

STEP 3 **Write a rough draft.**

Write your essay. Use your outline from Step 2. Include vocabulary from the unit where possible.

STEP 4 **Revise your rough draft.**

Read your essay. Use the Writing Checklist to look for mistakes. Work alone or in pairs.

Writing Checklist

- ❑ Does your introduction give background information about the people or place the problem affects?
- ❑ Does your introduction have a clear thesis statement that identifies the main problem and indicates the essay will give solutions?
- ❑ Do your body paragraphs support your thesis statement?
- ❑ Does your conclusion have a restated thesis?
- ❑ Did you use the coherence markers *this/these* + noun appropriately in your writing?

STEP 5 **Edit your writing.**

A. Edit your essay. Use the correction symbols chart on page 173. Correct any mistakes in capitalization, punctuation, spelling, verb tense, or the use of articles.

General statements with most plural count nouns do not use *the*.

EXAMPLE

ARTICLE
| B s y
~~The b~~iologist^ studi~~es~~ plants and animals.

General statements with non-count nouns do not use *the*.

EXAMPLE

ARTICLE
| P
~~The p~~ollution can have many effects on people.

B. Work in pairs. Exchange essays and check each other's work.

STEP 6 **Write a final copy.**

Correct your mistakes. Copy your final essay and give it to your instructor.

UNIT

4

Fact or Fiction?

In this unit you will:

- read articles about good luck charms, Bigfoot, and the Loch Ness monster
- learn how to annotate a reading
- learn to write an effective summary

PRE-READING 1

Discussion

Discuss the questions in pairs or small groups.

1. Do you believe in luck? Why or why not?
2. Do you (or does someone you know) have a lucky object? Why is the object important to you?
3. Do you think success comes more from luck or hard work? Explain.

Vocabulary

Read the boldfaced words and their definitions. Then complete the paragraph with the correct words. Change the form of words as needed.

associate with:	make a connection in your mind between one thing or person and another
attempt:	an act of trying to do something, especially something difficult
judgment:	an opinion that you form, especially after thinking carefully about something
odds:	chances that something will or will not happen
raise the question:	introduce an issue, or topic
superstition:	a belief that some objects or actions are lucky and some are unlucky or cause particular results

What's Your (Un)lucky Number?

Many cultures have (1) __superstitions__ about the number 13. It is a number that many people (2) __associate with__ bad luck. For example, race car drivers do not want the number 13 on their cars. They think using the number will decrease their (3) __odds__ of winning races. In addition, many office buildings and large hotels do not have a "13th floor." Calling this floor 12a or 12b is a(n) (4) __attempt__ to make their customers feel less worried. All of these behaviors (5) __raise the question__: is the number 13 unlucky, or is it a silly belief? It all depends on who you talk to. Everyone must make his or her own (6) __judgment__ about whether this number is bad luck or not.

READING SKILL

Annotating a Reading

Annotating means taking notes about important ideas while you are reading a text. Taking notes while you read will make you a more active and successful reader. Readers use both in-text annotations and side-text annotations.

In-text annotations are underlining or circling important ideas in the reading itself. When you annotate in-text, mark the words or phrases that help you identify and remember the ideas. Try not to underline or circle entire sentences or multiple sentences. In-text annotations often identify main ideas, examples, explanations, names, and terms.

Side-text annotations are writing ideas in the margins around the text. Side-text annotations record your own thoughts and reactions to what you read. Side-text annotations often emphasize ideas or words you think are very important, show relationships between ideas, summarize paragraphs or longer sections of text in your own words, and ask personal questions you have about the ideas in the text.

Look at the following paragraph from Reading 1, "Lucky Charms." Notice in-text and side-text annotations the reader has used.

**superstitions = coping mech.*

help w/ feelings ex. fear, anxiety, Ø control

Why is emotion always more powerful?

emotion + powfl. than thinking

Richard Lustberg, a Long Island psychologist who studies sports superstitions, says superstitions are "coping mechanisms." They can serve as help for some who experience fear, anxiety, or loss of control in a world where the odds aren't necessarily in their favor, he says. "Intellectually, people understand that it doesn't make sense, but emotionally they're unable to make the break," he says. "Emotion always overruns intelligence, otherwise we'd have world peace, right?"

Symbols and Abbreviations Readers often use their own symbols and abbreviations to keep their side-text annotations short. Here are some common symbols and abbreviations readers use for annotating.

SYMBOL/ ABBREVIATION	MEANING
*	important
=	is/are, means, is equal to
≠	not equal to
Ø	not, no, don't/doesn't, didn't, won't, loss of
+	more
<	increase
ex.	example
imp.	important
info	information
b/c	because
w/	with

Notice these examples from the annotated paragraph.

EXAMPLE ANNOTATIONS	MEANING
*superstitions = coping **mech.**	Important: Superstitions are coping mechanisms.
help **w/**feelings	Superstitions help people with certain feelings.
ex: fear, anxiety, **Ø** control	For example: fear, anxiety, and loss of control
Emotion **+ powfl.** than thinking	Emotion is more powerful than thinking.

Practice

Read the article and take notes using in-text and side-text annotations. Use symbols and abbreviations where possible.

READING 1

Lucky Charms

1 All of our sciences and technologies explain a lot of things—why the sky is blue, the grass is green, and how, for instance, chemical reactions behave differently without gravity. But they won't explain why Jo Finning won't play bingo[1] without bringing along her large brass bell. "You want to be lucky," says Finning, of Green Island. In the bingo halls, the racetrack, in fishing boats, bowling alleys, you name it, **superstitions** and good luck charms are embraced—usually against people's own good **judgment**.

2 Underneath his team-issued black socks, Tri-City Valley Cats pitcher[2] Casey Brown has been wearing the same pair of socks all season. For good luck, he says. What about pitching without his lucky socks? "No, I always wear the socks," he says, pulling his cap down tight around his head. This **raises the question**: Do good-luck charms work? Of course not—unless they do.

3 For the Mexican Olympic team, they didn't. The team headed to

[1] **bingo:** a game played for money or prizes in which you win if a set of numbers chosen by chance are the same as one of the lines of numbers on your card

[2] **pitcher:** the player in baseball who throws the ball to the batter

Athens in the summer of 2004 with charms, amulets,[3] and religious items. But when the games closed, Mexico only took home four medals, well below expectations. For swimmer Gary Hall Jr., they do work. Against U.S. Olympic policy, he wore his good-luck robe and swimming trunks to team events rather than team gear. Because he did—or not because he did—the aging underdog[4] was a gold-medal winner in the 50-meter freestyle.

4 Believe in them or not, good-luck charms and superstitions have been an essential part of human life throughout history, says Donald Dossey, a psychologist and superstition expert from Asheville, N.C. "Superstitious behavior is really an **attempt** to control the universe that is way too powerful for us to control," he says.

5 In fact, being superstitious could be in our nature. The famous psychologist B. F. Skinner said he proved superstitious behavior can be created in animals. When an animal is placed in a box and food is dispensed every five minutes, the animal will develop a pattern of behavior that it **associates with** the delivery of food. For instance, if the animal just happens to lift a foot just as the food is dispensed, it will repeat this behavior, which will be sporadically[5] reinforced.

6 Today, Chris Caruso continues to use her good-luck charm when she plays bingo at the Italian Community Center in Troy. Her charm is a Mother's Day card from her son, which she displays side by side with her bingo cards and marker. "Sometimes it works, and sometimes it doesn't," says Caruso, of Watervliet.

7 Richard Lustberg, a Long Island psychologist who studies sports superstitions, says superstitions are "coping mechanisms."[6] "They can serve as help for some who experience fear, anxiety, or loss of control in a world where the **odds** are not necessarily in their favor. Intellectually, people understand that it doesn't make sense, but emotionally they're unable to make the break,"[7] he says. "Emotion always overruns[8] intelligence, otherwise we'd have world peace, right?"

[3] **amulet:** a small piece of jewelry worn to protect against bad luck, disease, etc.

[4] **underdog:** a person or team in a competition that is expected to lose

[5] **sporadically:** not happening in regular or continuous way

[6] **coping mechanism:** a way of behaving that helps you to avoid or deal with something that is difficult or dangerous

[7] **make the break:** to accept that there is no connection between two things

[8] **overrun:** take control over something

Identifying Main Ideas

Use your annotations to help you answer the questions below. Mark the statements* M *(main idea) or* S *(supporting idea).

___ 1. Science can't explain why people believe in good-luck charms.

___ 2. People believe in good-luck charms despite no proof that they actually work.

___ 3. Jo Finning uses a good-luck charm when she plays bingo.

____ 4. Carrying lucky charms to the Olympics did not help the Mexican Olympic team win a lot of medals.

____ 5. Many athletes carry good-luck charms to help them win competitions or games.

____ 6. According to psychologists, being superstitious could be in our nature.

____ 7. Psychologist B. F. Skinner studied superstitious behavior in animals.

____ 8. Psychologist Richard Lustberg believes good-luck charms help people cope with difficult situations.

Identifying Details

Scan Reading 1. Match the good-luck charms to the people associated with them.

____ 1. Casey Brown	a. charms, amulets, and religious items
____ 2. Mexican Olympic team	b. a Mother's Day card
____ 3. Gary Hall Jr.	c. a robe and swimming trunks
____ 4. Chris Caruso	d. a pair of socks

Making Inferences

The writer's feelings about good-luck charms are not stated directly in the reading. Check (✓) one feeling in each pair that the writer seems to convey.

1. ☐ sure ☐ uncertain
2. ☐ serious ☐ cheerful
3. ☐ curious ☐ uninterested

VOCABULARY SKILL

Using Collocations with *Do* and *Make*

The verbs *do* and *make* collocate (go together) with different nouns.

EXAMPLES

Correct	make a correction	make a change
Incorrect	do a correction	do a change
Correct	do a job	do work
Incorrect	make a job	make work

Practice

A. ***These nouns collocate with*** make ***or*** do. ***Write the correct verb. If necessary, use a dictionary.***

1. make an attempt
2. make a connection
3. do business
4. make a choice
5. do a favor
6. make plans
7. make a suggestion
8. do research

B. ***Complete each sentence with the correct form of*** make ***or*** do. ***Then mark each sentence*** A (agree) ***or*** D (disagree) ***and discuss your answers in pairs.***

D 1. It was easy for me to make the decision to learn English.

D 2. It is important to make mistakes when learning a new language.

A 3. I learn better when I do homework with classmates.

A 4. I have done a lot of progress with my English.

D 5. Friends always do favors for friends.

FROM READING TO WRITING

Journal
Choose one of your answers and write a journal entry.

Reflecting on the Reading

Discuss the questions in pairs or small groups.

1. Do you think good-luck charms work? Why or why not?
2. In your native country or another country you've visited, what kinds of objects are considered lucky? Why?

PRE-READING 2

Discussion

Discuss the questions in pairs or small groups.

1. Many Americans believe black cats are unlucky. Are there any animals that you consider lucky or unlucky? Explain.
2. Many popular movies have been made about imaginary creatures and animals. Why do people like to watch these kinds of movies?

Vocabulary

Read the article. Match each boldfaced word or phrase with the definition in the box. Write the letter.

The Yeti

For more than 50 years, scientists and explorers have been studying an **extraordinary** (1___) creature called the yeti. This creature is like no other living thing. The animal **is confined** (2___) to a small region of the cold Himalayan Mountains. Scientists believe it might **be related** (3___) **to** apes because its body is covered with hair, and it can stand on two legs.

However, the Yeti might not even be real. This mysterious creature has caused a lot of **controversy** (4___). People disagree on whether it truly exists. So far, scientists haven't found enough **conclusive** (5___) evidence to prove its existence. Because there are no pictures or videos of it, many people **deny** (6___) that the Yeti is a real creature. They think it is just an ordinary animal, such as a large bear.

a. be connected to another thing in some way
b. no doubt that something is true
c. say that something is not true, or that you do not believe something
d. in only one place or time
e. very unusual or surprising
f. a serious argument or disagreement among many people over a plan, decision, etc. over a long period of time

Legendary Creatures

1 King Kong[1] and Godzilla[2] are two of the most recognized characters in film. Everyone knows that they are not real, but what would happen if people actually came across such fantastic creatures in real life? Cryptozoologists are scientists who believe such **extraordinary** monster-like animals do live on earth, and for decades they have focused most of their attention on two bizarre but fascinating creatures—Bigfoot and the Loch Ness monster. Today, there is **controversy** about whether these legendary animals belong to science or science fiction.[3]

2 Since the early 1920s, there have been hundreds of sightings of Bigfoot in the northwestern United States. Most witnesses describe Bigfoot, also known as Sasquatch, as a 7- to 9-foot ape-like creature that is covered in dark brown or reddish hair. Although some people claim to have seen Bigfoot, most reports are about the footprints it leaves behind. According to ecologist Robert Michael Pyle, the "tracks commonly measure 15 to 20 inches or more in length." These enormous footprints give the creature its name.

3 Bigfoot sightings **are** not **confined to** the United States. There have been accounts of similar beasts in Asia, Australia, and South America. Most occur in the wilderness, usually near rivers, lakes, and creeks, and cryptozoologists suggest that this common habitat is evidence for Bigfoot being a true species.[4] However, many scientists are not convinced, for no one has ever found a fossil that matches the animal's description. Many believe Bigfoot is a hoax,[5] but scientists continue to study the beast, and sightings continue to occur. Many movies star the creature, and Bigfoot has become an unforgettable character in children's literature and cartoons.

4 In the waters of the Scottish lake Loch Ness lives another creature of controversy. The Loch Ness monster, also nicknamed Nessie or Ness by locals, has been popular since the 1930s. Witnesses of the monster give similar descriptions: It is between 20 and 25 feet long, and it has a long, narrow neck. Some say it has short flippers similar to those of a dolphin. One theory is that the Loch Ness monster **is related to** the plesiosaur, an aquatic[6] reptile with a long neck that lived with the dinosaurs millions of years ago.

5 Since the 1960s, scientists have tried to prove and disprove the existence of Nessie. Earlier attempts consisted of photographs of the monster; however, many people believe the photos were fakes. Scientists have also

(continued)

[1] **King Kong:** a very large gorilla that is the main character in the film *King Kong* (1933 and 2005)
[2] **Godzilla:** a very large monster-like dinosaur featured in a number of Japanese films
[3] **science fiction:** a type of writing that describes imaginary future developments in science and their effect on life, for example traveling in time or to other planets with life on them

[4] **species:** a group of animals or plants which are all similar and can breed together to produce young animals or plants of the same kind as them
[5] **hoax:** an attempt to make people believe something that is not true
[6] **aquatic:** living or growing in water

used sonar[7] technology to locate the monster. One group of scientists identified a large creature in the lake, perhaps up to 20 feet long, but they never saw it with their own eyes. Scientists have also used microphones to try to "hear" Nessie. Despite the lack of **conclusive** evidence, many people still believe (or want to believe) in the possibility of the Loch Ness monster. Nessie has not only appeared as a character in numerous books, television shows, movies, and computer games, but has also brought many millions of dollars to Scotland's tourist industry.

6 The question still remains: Are these creatures fact or fiction? No one has proven they definitely exist, yet no one has entirely disproved their existence. Either way, no one can **deny** their impact on the world. Just like King Kong and Godzilla, Bigfoot and the Loch Ness monster have become part of popular culture, and they will continue to capture both children's and adult's imaginations for years to come.

[7] **sonar:** equipment on a ship that uses sound waves to find out the position of objects under the water

Identifying Main Ideas

Match the main points from the box with each set of details in the chart.

evidence description ~~location~~ other names popular culture

	Bigfoot	The Loch Ness Monster
1) location	• northwestern U.S. • Asia, Australia, S. America	• Scotland
2) other names	• Sasquatch	• Nessie or Ness
3) description	• 7- to 9-foot ape-like creature • dark brown or reddish hair	• 20–25 feet long • long, narrow neck • short flippers
4) evidence	• some have seen Bigfoot • most reports from footprints it leaves behind	• photos • sonar technology has located a large creature in Loch Ness
5) Popular culture	• character in movies, children's literature, and cartoons	• subject in literature, television, movies, and computer games

Identifying Details

Answer the questions.

1. What is a cryptozoologist?
2. According to scientists, what kind of habitat does Bigfoot live in?
3. When did the Loch Ness monster first become popular?
4. According to one theory, which reptile is the Loch Ness monster related to?

Making Inferences

Infer what the writer would say is true even though it is not directly stated in the reading. Check (✓) each statement that the author would agree with.

✓ 1. It is difficult to prove that Bigfoot and Nessie exist.

✓ 2. The same evidence can be understood by scientists in different ways.

____ 3. Bigfoot is more difficult to witness than the Loch Ness monster.

____ 4. All scientists believe the Loch Ness monster is a plesiosaur.

FROM READING TO WRITING

Journal
Choose one of your answers and write a journal entry.

Reflecting on the Reading

Discuss the questions in pairs or groups.

1. Have you heard of other creatures that are similar to Bigfoot?
2. Do you believe Bigfoot and Nessie really exist? Why or why not?
3. Why do you think that stories about legendary creatures like Bigfoot and the Loch Ness monster are so popular?

WRITING

WRITING SKILL

Vocabulary
For more practice with vocabulary, go to pages 180–181.

Writing a Summary

Summarizing a text shows that you have understood it. When you summarize, you state the main idea of a reading and its main points. The length of a summary can vary; a summary of an article is usually one paragraph, while a summary of a book can be one or two pages.

When writing a summary of an article, follow these steps:

- **The first sentence should identify the title or author of the article, and state the article's main idea.**

EXAMPLE

"Can Cell-Phone Recycling Help African Gorillas?" reports that people can help African gorillas survive by recycling their cell phones.

- **The remaining sentences should state the main points of the article.**
- **Paraphrase the author's ideas in your own words without changing their meaning.**
- **Only include details from the article if they are necessary to understand the main ideas.**
- **Do not include any personal information or opinions.**

Before writing a summary, it is helpful to list the main points of the reading. Use *Wh*-questions (*Who?*, *What?*, *When?*, *Where?*, *Why?*, and *How?*) to help you identify these points. For example, look at this sample list for the article "Lucky Charms," pp. 62–63.

- *Who?*

  psychologists, athletes & people
- *What?*

  good-luck charms

  no scientific proof as support
- *When?*

  Athletes use them during games.

  People use them in uncontrollable situations.
- *Why?*

  to help people cope emotionally in difficult situations

Practice

A. ***Read the summaries of Reading 1, "Lucky Charms." Then complete the chart that follows. Check (✔) the information that is true for each summary.***

Summary 1 "Lucky Charms" discusses why science can't explain good-luck charms. A lot of people use good-luck charms in their lives, especially during important events. Students sometimes carry good-luck charms with them when they take tests in school. Many of my friends believe in this superstition, but in my judgment, objects cannot bring you good luck. I think success comes only from working hard.

Summary 2 In this article, the author explains when and why people use good-luck charms. Many athletes use good luck charms. Pitcher Casey Brown wears the same socks at every game because he associates them with good luck. Swimmer Gary Hall Jr. wore a good-luck robe and swimming trunks to improve his odds at the Olympics, and he won a gold medal. Chris Caruso brings a Mother's Day card from her son to help bring her luck when she plays bingo.

Summary 3 In "Lucky Charms," the author reports that people carry lucky charms even though there is no conclusive evidence that they work. Some athletes carry good-luck charms during competitions, hoping they will help them win. Psychologists believe athletes, and people in general, use good-luck charms in situations that they can't control. They believe lucky charms help people cope better emotionally in difficult situations.

		SUMMARY 1	SUMMARY 2	SUMMARY 3
POSITIVE	States the author or title	✔		
	Includes the main idea			
	Includes the main points			
NEGATIVE	Gives too many details			
	Gives new information			
	Includes personal opinions			

B. Which summary is the most effective? Compare your answers in pairs.

WRITING ASSIGNMENT

Write a one-paragraph summary of Reading 2, "Legendary Creatures." Follow the steps.

STEP 1 **Get ideas.**

Scan Reading 2 and review your in-text and side-text annotations. Use *Wh-* questions to help you identify the article's main idea and key points.

STEP 2 **Organize your ideas.**

Write the first sentence of your summary. Then list the main points in logical order.

In "Legendary Creatures," the author discusses

1. ______________________________
2. ______________________________
3. ______________________________
4. ______________________________

STEP 3 **Write a rough draft.**

Write your summary. Use your outline from Step 2.

STEP 4 **Revise your rough draft.**

Read your summary. Use the Writing Checklist to look for mistakes. Work alone or in pairs.

Writing Checklist

- ❑ Does your summary identify the title and author of the article?
- ❑ Does your summary include only the article's main idea and main points?
- ❑ Did you use your own words?
- ❑ Did you use vocabulary from the unit appropriately?
- ❑ Did you NOT include personal information or opinions?

STEP 5 **Edit your writing.**

A. Edit your paragraph. Use the correction symbols chart on page 173. Correct any mistakes in capitalization, punctuation, spelling, verb-tense, or transition signals.

Transition signals, such as *therefore*, *however*, and *in addition*, usually follow a semicolon (;) or period (.). The signals are followed by a comma (,).

EXAMPLE

No one has found physical evidence like a fossil, of Bigfoot.

TRANSITION SIGNAL

therefore, many scientists don't believe it exists.

B. Work in pairs. Exchange paragraphs and check each other's work.

STEP 6 **Write a final copy.**

Correct your mistakes. Copy your final paragraph and give it to your instructor.

UNIT

5

Personality

In this unit you will:

- read articles about musical personalities and types of stress
- learn to recognize classification markers
- organize and write a classification essay

PRE-READING 1

Discussion

Discuss the questions in pairs or small groups.

1. Look at the picture. What kind of music makes *you* happy?
2. Put this list of activities in order from the most enjoyable to the least enjoyable: listening to music, watching TV, shopping, going to the movies, and reading.

Vocabulary

Read the sentences. Match the boldfaced words with the definitions in the box.

____ 1. Some people believe that listening to classical music can make children smarter. Others disagree with this **hypothesis** because there isn't enough proof.

____ 2. American culture often **categorizes** people by their age. For instance, pre-teens are children aged 8–12, teens are aged 13–17, and adults are 18 and over.

____ 3. The clothes people wear often **reveal** what kind of job they have. For example, businesspeople usually wear suits, and doctors often wear white coats.

____ 4. There are two **distinct** types of undergraduate degrees offered at American colleges: an Associate's (two-year), and a Bachelor's (four-year) degree.

____ 5. Academic clubs at colleges can **complement** your studies. Being involved in one can add to your knowledge about a subject.

____ 6. Psychologists have determined that people **tend to** make friends with people who are similar to them.

____ 7. Sandy is a very quiet person, preferring to spend time at home. Her **extroverted** sister, Joanne, is the opposite. She prefers to be with friends.

____ 8. Social **interaction** is easier with friends. In contrast, talking to strangers or people you've only just met can sometimes be uncomfortable.

____ 9. Even though Great Britain and the United States are very different, there is some **overlap** between their cultures. For example, both believe it is important to be on time.

____ 10. Although people think crime is rising, violent crime in some cities is dropping. City officials are still unsure of what **accounts for** this decline.

a. classify people or things in groups according to what type they are, or say which group they are in
b. accompany, complete, or perfect something else in a pleasing way
c. an idea that is suggested as an explanation for something but that has not yet been proven to be true
d. the degree to which two things or activities share similar features
e. give a satisfactory explanation of why something has happened or why something was done
f. clearly different or separate
g. do a particular thing often and be likely to do it again
h. confident and enjoying being with other people
i. make known something that was previously secret or unknown
j. the activity of talking to other people, working together with them, etc.

READING 1

Musical Personalities

1 How important is the music we listen to? According to psychologists Peter J. Rentfrow and Samuel D. Gosling, it might be more important than we realize. Rentfrow and Gosling came up with the **hypothesis** that people choose music that reflects the kind of person they are. In other words, these researchers believe that our music preferences are tied to[1] our personality type. In order to test this hypothesis, the psychologists interviewed undergraduate students at the University of Texas at Austin to see if they could **categorize** the students by their "musical personality."

2 Their research, which appeared in the *Journal of Personality and Social Psychology*, led to some very interesting discoveries. The undergraduate students rated music to be as important to their lives as other hobbies and activities. Music was even more important than the television shows they watched and the types of food they ate. In addition, the researchers found that the students "believed that their music preferences **revealed** a substantial[2] amount of information about their own personalities . . . and the personalities of other people." But perhaps most interestingly, Rentfrow and Gosling began to see patterns when they looked at the link between music preference and personality type. Their conclusion was that people could be categorized into four **distinct** musical personalities.

Reflective and Complex

3 According to the study, people who enjoy blues, folk, jazz, or classical music are open to[3] new experiences, consider themselves

(continued)

[1] **be tied to:** be related to something and dependent on it

[2] **substantial:** large in amount or number

[3] **be open to:** be willing to consider something new or accept something new

intelligent, have active imaginations, and are good conversationalists. Reflective and Complex people appreciate the slower pace and complexity of these four musical styles because they match their relaxed, intellectual personality.

Intense and Rebellious

4 People in this personality category also welcome new experiences. Like the Reflective and Complex, they consider themselves smart and enjoy the company of others. However, they do have two characteristics that make them unique: they are more athletic, and they get pleasure from taking risks. These thrill-seekers[4] like high-energy music, including alternative rock, heavy metal, and hard rock. The power of the electric guitars in these music styles **complements** the intensity of this group's personality. Rentfrow and Gosling's study also showed that these people connected to the lyrics in these rock songs, which often spoke about rebellion, or resisting rules and authority.[5]

Upbeat and Conventional

5 Many people fit this personality type, including fans of both pop and country music. These people prefer simple music that is upbeat or happy. Those who like the lyrics of pop and country **tend to** be more conservative, or more resistant to change and new experiences. They value tradition, and though they are not big risk-takers, they do enjoy being physically active. Like their music, they are cheerful people. The Upbeat and Conventional enjoy being social, and they take pleasure in hanging out with[6] and helping other people.

[4] **thrill-seeker:** someone who does things that are dangerous because they like the feeling of excitement it gives them

[5] **authority:** the power you have because of your official position or because people respect your knowledge and experience

[6] **hang out with:** spend a lot of time with people

Energetic and Rhythmic

6 Last but not least are the fans of rap, funk, and dance music. Like their music, these people are full of energy. They are enthusiastic and outgoing, both physically and socially. The Energetic and Rhythmic are **extroverted**, and they love social **interaction**. They tend to be talkative and are what some people might call the "life of the party." They also don't like to keep their emotions hidden. They prefer to express their feelings to others immediately. Clearly, the electric instruments and rhythmic tempos of rap, funk, and dance suit[7] these lively people perfectly.

Conclusions

7 Rentfrow and Gosling were the first psychologists to categorize personalities by music choice. Their four personality types—Reflective and Complex, Intense and Rebellious, Upbeat and Conventional, and Energetic and Rhythmic—emerged from months of research into the ways college students felt about music. From their research, they concluded that "knowing what kind of music a person likes could serve as a clue to his or her personality." However, they caution that the four personality types are only guidelines.[8] Given the complex nature of human personalities and preferences, there will always be some **overlap**. Not all rock fans are risk-takers, for example, and not all extroverted people listen to rap. Plus, the researchers point out that the categories don't **account for** those people who enjoy listening to all different kinds of music. In fact, this may even lead to the description of a whole new personality type.

[7] **suit:** have the right qualities for a particular person, purpose, or situation

[8] **guideline:** something that helps you form an opinion or make a decision

Identifying Main Ideas

Answer the questions.

1. According to paragraph 1, what hypothesis did Rentfrow and Gosling try to prove?
2. How are the Reflective and Complex and the Intense and Rebellious types similar? How are they different?
3. What kind of musical personality do listeners of pop and country music have?
4. What is the main idea of paragraph 7?

Identifying Details

Mark the statements* T *(true) or* F *(false).

____ 1. Rentfrow and Gosling studied the music preferences of high school students.

____ 2. Rentfrow and Gosling's research showed that people believe listening to music is as important as other hobbies.

____ 3. People who listen to rock and heavy metal music are Energetic and Rhythmic.

____ 4. Upbeat and Conventional people do not like to take risks.

____ 5. Rentfrow and Gosling were the first psychologists to study musical personalities.

Making Inferences

This information is not stated directly. Check (✔) the information that can be inferred about each personality type in Reading 1.

Personality Types and Behaviors

	REFLECTIVE AND COMPLEX	INTENSE AND REBELLIOUS	UPBEAT AND CONVENTIONAL	ENERGETIC AND RHYTHMIC
1. traveling to foreign countries	✔			
2. participating in sports				
3. going to parties				

Recognizing Classification Markers

When writers classify information, they identify a general topic and divide it into types. The author of Reading 1, for example, identified the larger topic of *musical personalities* and broke this concept down into four different *types* of musical personalities:

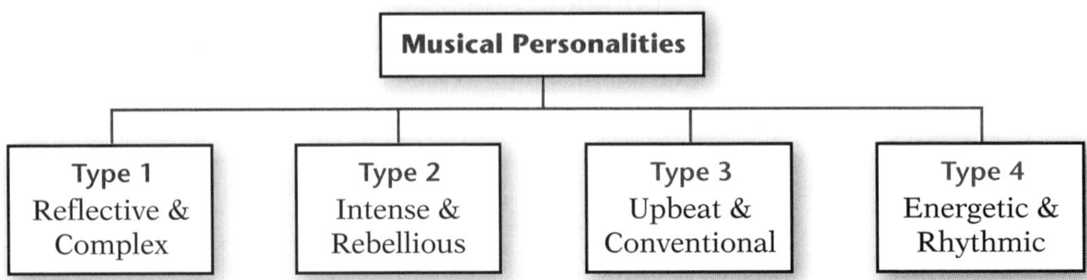

Classification markers are words that help readers identify when a topic is being divided into types. Notice the classification markers the author of Reading 1 uses.

> Rentfrow and Gosling were the first psychologists to categorize personalities by music choice. Their four personality types—*Reflective and Complex, Intense and Rebellious, Upbeat and Conventional,* and *Energetic and Rhythmic*—emerged from months of research into the ways college students felt about music.

Recognizing classification markers will help you better understand how and when writers classify a topic into smaller topics. The chart below lists classification markers writers often use.

VERBS	NOUNS	
categorize	category	kind
classify	class	part
distinguish	genre	style
divide	division	sort
group	group	type

Practice

Read the sentences. Circle the classification markers. Then complete the diagrams.

1. Pop music is one of the most popular musical (styles) in the world. Rock and hip-hop are perhaps the most well-known genres of pop music. Two other popular styles are R&B (rhythm and blues) and country music.

2. Long-term memories are memories that people remember for a long time. They can be divided into three main types. Episodic memories are memories we have about specific events, such as a wedding day. Semantic memories are facts we have learned, like knowing the meanings of words. The third group of memories is called procedural memories. They are memories of skills our body has learned to do, like driving a car or writing our name.

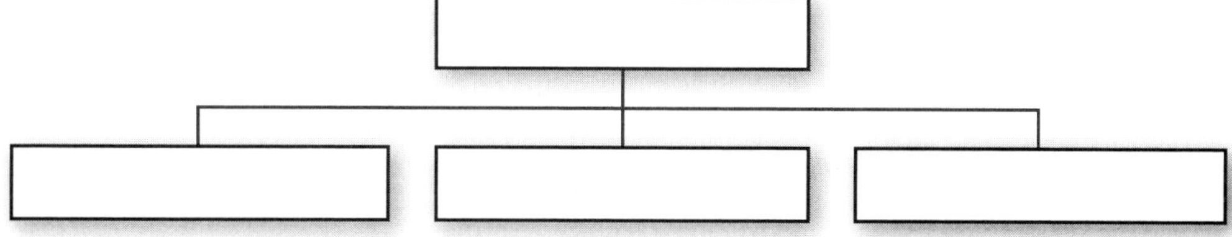

VOCABULARY SKILL

Using Verb Suffixes

Suffixes can be added to the end of certain nouns and adjectives to change them into verbs. For example, the noun *category* becomes the verb *categorize* by adding the suffix *-ize*.

EXAMPLE

Rentfrow and Gosling categorized personalities based on musical preferences.

The suffixes *-ize*, *-en*, *-ify*, and *-ate* mean "make." The chart below shows how these four suffixes can be added to nouns and adjectives to change them into verbs.

-ize		
category (n.)	➛	categorize (make categories)*
hypothesis (n.)	➛	hypothesize (make a hypothesis)*
-en		
length (n.)	➛	lengthen (make longer)
strength (n.)	➛	strengthen (make stronger)
-ify		
class (n.)	➛	classify (make classes or categories)
clear (adj.)	➛	clarify (make clear)*
-ate		
valid (adj.)	➛	validate (make valid)
active (adj.)	➛	activate (make active)*

*some words have spelling changes

Practice

Circle the correct form of the word to complete each sentence.

1. After months of research, the scientists learned that their original (hypothesize / hypothesis) was incorrect.
2. Psychologists believe that when we first meet people, we (category / categorize) them based on what they are wearing and what they say.
3. Some people think that keeping (strong / strengthen) relationships with others can actually (length / lengthen) a person's life.
4. One way to (class / classify) people is by their age. Another way is by their ethnicity.
5. Patricia had to (clear / clarify) how she felt because her friend misunderstood her.

6. Some people like to do low-energy activities like reading or playing computer games. Others like to be more (active / activate), preferring sports and outdoor activities.
7. Sometimes researchers need to repeat an experiment many times in order to (valid / validate) their results.

FROM READING TO WRITING

Reflecting on the Reading

Journal
Choose one of your answers and write a journal entry.

Discuss the questions in pairs or small groups.

1. According to the categories in Reading 1, which personality type would Rentfrow and Gosling say you have? Do you agree that you have this personality? Explain.
2. Discuss one song or musician that is important to you. Why does this song or musician have special meaning for you?

PRE-READING 2

Discussion

Discuss the questions in pairs or small groups.

1. Can personality affect the amount of happiness a person feels? Explain.
2. Even happy events, like getting married or getting a new job, can cause stress. Have you (or has someone you know) ever felt stress during a happy event? Explain.

Vocabulary

Read the boldfaced words and their definitions. Then complete the paragraph with the correct words or phrases. Change the form of words as needed.

adapt to:	gradually change behavior and ideas to fit a new situation
circumstances:	the facts or conditions that affect a situation, action, event, etc.
confirm:	show that something is definitely true, especially by providing more proof
encounter:	experience problems, difficulties, or opposition when you are trying to do something
excessive:	much more than is reasonable or necessary
enhance:	make something better
ensure:	make certain that something will happen
predominantly:	mostly or mainly

Reverse Culture Shock

Studying in a foreign country can (1) ________________ people's lives in many ways. They try new foods, meet interesting people, and often learn to speak another language.

When people study abroad, they can often feel culture shock as well. Culture shock happens (2) ________________ to people who travel or move to a new country. However, research has (3) ________________ that people can feel a different form of culture shock when they return home as well; this is called "reverse culture shock."

When people live in a new country for a long time, they must learn to (4) ________________ new (5) ________________. They have to live differently from the way they did at home. When they return home, they often feel that "everything has changed," but they don't know why.

To help (6) ________________ that people don't feel a(n) (7) ________________ amount of reverse culture shock, psychologists suggest being prepared for the changes. First, people should remember that they are not alone; almost everyone will (8) ________________ some problems when they return home. Also, people should not assume everything will be the same, and should talk often with friends and family about how they are feeling.

Eustress or You Stress?

1 "Change is good," or so the saying goes. According to psychologists Charles G. Morris and Albert A. Maistro, people actually dislike change because it threatens a natural desire to keep things the way they are. They state, "Most people have a strong preference for order, continuity,[1] and predictability[2] in their lives. Therefore, anything, good or bad, that requires change can be experienced as stressful. The more change required, the more stressful the situation." Everybody feels stress, but not all stress is the same. Psychologists distinguish between two types of stress: good stress, called *eustress*, and bad stress, called *distress*—and which one we feel may depend on the type of personality we have.

Eustress

2 Many people would probably be surprised that stress can benefit you and your body, but that is exactly what eustress does. This stress is not only good for you; it is actually designed to help you survive. When humans **encounter** a dangerous situation, their breathing becomes faster, their heart rate increases, and their throat and nose muscles open up to allow more air to get to the lungs. This physical reaction is called the *fight-or-flight response*, and it prepares the body either to fight the danger or to escape it. For example, if you were alone on the street and encountered a stranger late at night, your body might prepare your heart and lungs to help you run away as quickly as possible from the danger. Without eustress, you would never get this head start.[3]

3 Eustress does not occur only in dangerous **circumstances**, however. Anytime we are required to perform, the same physical reactions take place to help us handle the situation. For example, when runners are about to race in a marathon,[4] eustress gives them optimal[5] strength for the race by pumping more blood to their muscles. Public speakers feel this same kind of stress just before giving a speech, and feeling nervous actually helps them concentrate and perform better. The stress is not a punishment—it is there to help people do their best.

Distress

4 Distress, or bad stress, is the opposite of eustress. People often feel distress when they experience a major change in their life, such as a divorce or the loss of a loved one. Distress can have negative effects on the body, including headaches, stomach pain, and muscle pain, and it can even weaken our immune system, which is the part of the body responsible for fighting illnesses. Studies on college students have **confirmed** this, showing that students are more likely to get sick during finals week because of the stress associated with studying for such important exams.

(continued)

[1] **continuity:** the state of continuing over a long period of time without being interrupted or changing

[2] **predictability:** the state of behaving or happening in a way that you expect

[3] **head start:** an advantage that helps you to be successful

[4] **marathon:** a long race in which competitors run 26 miles (42 kilometers)

[5] **optimal:** the best or most appropriate

5 Distress also reveals itself emotionally. With too much of it, people can become angry, frustrated, or depressed. Very often, feelings of anger and frustration are caused by the hassles[6] of everyday life, like waiting in long lines or sitting in traffic for too long. In addition, conflicts with others, such as arguments with friends or loved ones, can lead to negative stress. People can also feel conflict between two or more demands, needs, or goals. For instance, those students who must decide to work or study full-time can feel distress because they desire to do both but are forced to give up one or the other.

Stress and Personality

6 Distinguishing between which kind of stress we feel can sometimes be tricky. Stress is sometimes meant to benefit us, but this does not always happen. Some students find that the stress from taking tests **enhances** their performance, while others find that test taking makes them forget everything they know. Why is this? Whether we feel stress as eustress or distress depends on more than just the situation. Psychologists note that the type of stress we feel is also tied to the kind of personality we have—Type A or Type B.

7 People with a Type A personality frequently feel distress. They tend to be very competitive, and are often labeled "workaholics" because they devote so much time and energy to their work in order to **ensure** their success. Unfortunately, focusing so much on work and deadlines can make them feel **excessive** amounts of distress, which makes it difficult for them to relax. Everyone is confronted with stressful situations, but the distress Type A people feel comes **predominantly** from themselves because they are naturally more impatient and uptight.[7] People with Type B personalities are the exact opposite: more relaxed and easygoing. While the Type A person would become very upset sitting in a traffic jam, the Type B would not let the situation control how he or she feels. Because these people find it easier to **adapt to** change, they are able to deal with stress in a more positive and effective way, which results in their experiencing more eustress than distress.

8 Stress is both internal and external. Sometimes we can't control what happens to us, but we can control how we react to stressful situations. With the right attitude and determination, people can convert[8] distress into eustress and make their lives happier as a result.

[6] **hassle:** something that is annoying because it causes problems or is difficult to do

[7] **uptight:** unable to relax

[8] **convert:** change something into a different form or thing

Identifying Main Ideas

Read each question. Circle the letter of the best answer.

1. What is the main idea of the reading?
   a. People feel stress when they have to perform or when there is a change to their daily life.
   b. Even though all people feel eustress and distress, personality can affect how much of each type of stress we feel.

c. People with a Type A personality feel more distress than eustress because they can't adapt to change easily.

d. Students feel more stress than other people because of the pressure associated with taking tests.

2. What is the main idea of paragraph 2?
   a. Eustress is good stress that can help people survive.
   b. The *fight-or-flight response* is a physical reaction.
   c. Heart rate increases when people feel eustress.
   d. People feel eustress when they encounter strangers.

3. What is the main idea of paragraph 4?
   a. Many college and university students get sick during finals week.
   b. The immune system is the part of the body that fights illnesses.
   c. People can get headaches and muscle pain when they feel distress.
   d. Distress can cause pain and make it easier for people to get sick.

4. What is the main idea of paragraph 5?
   a. Conflicts and daily hassles can cause people to feel distress.
   b. Sitting in traffic and waiting in long lines is frustrating.
   c. Students feel distress when making important decisions.
   d. People feel angry and frustrated when arguing with friends.

5. What is the main idea of paragraph 7?
   a. Type A people are impatient, and they find it difficult to relax.
   b. People with a Type B personality are relaxed and easygoing.
   c. Type A people tend to feel more distress than Type B people.
   d. It is difficult to control how much negative stress people feel.

Identifying Details

Answer the questions.

1. What happens to the body during the *fight-or-flight response*?
2. How does eustress help runners be physically prepared for a race?
3. What effects can distress have on the body?

Making Inferences

What meaning can be inferred from the sentence? Circle the letter of the best answer.

1. People actually dislike change because it threatens a natural desire to keep things the way they are.
   a. It is normal for people to resist change.
   b. It is difficult to make people change.
   c. Change can be both good and bad.
2. Many people would probably be surprised that stress can benefit you and your body, but that's exactly what eustress does.
   a. Stress can affect the body in different ways.
   b. Eustress is the most common type of stress.
   c. People often assume that all stress is negative.
3. With the right attitude and determination, people can convert distress into eustress and make their lives happier as a result.
   a. People can't control the amount of stress they feel.
   b. With time, distress usually turns into eustress.
   c. Changing distress to eustress requires effort.

FROM READING TO WRITING

Journal
Choose one of your answers and write a journal entry.

Reflecting on the Reading

Discuss the questions in pairs or small groups.

1. Which type of stress do you experience more often, "good stress" or "bad stress"? Explain and give examples.
2. Do you believe that people can be categorized into two personality groups, Type A and Type B? Why?

WRITING

Vocabulary
For more practice with vocabulary, go to pages 182–183.

The Classification Essay

Classification essays divide a topic into different types or groups and explain the characteristics of each type or group. Reading 1 categorized people into four musical personalities and described the characteristics of each group. In a similar way, Reading 2 focused on the topic of stress, divided it into two specific types of stress, eustress and distress, and explained the characteristics of each type. A psychology course may ask you to identify and discuss different kinds of intelligence; in a biology course, you might write about different types of plants or animals.

Read the model essay. What four types of bosses does the essay discuss?

MODEL

Four Typical Bosses

1 Just as there are many types of people in the world, there are also many different kinds of bosses. Most people will have to deal with more than one boss in their lives, and every boss has his or her own personality. Based on my own work experience, I can categorize bosses into four types: the lion, the bee, the cat, and the dog.

2 Lions know they are in charge, and they expect their employees to follow orders correctly the first time. Employees need to be careful not to make them angry because lions have bad tempers. These bosses are also extremely proud of their position, and they demand respect from everyone.

3 Bees are always buzzing around from one project to the next. Like lions, they are hard workers, and they do whatever it takes to get the job done. They are good role models for their employees because they are willing to work so hard. Unfortunately, however, sometimes bees are too busy to see what's going on around them, so their workers sometimes see them as unfriendly or uncaring.

4 The cat is more relaxed than the bee. Cats tend to be very independent, preferring to work alone. They often keep happy employees, for they don't bother them or stand over them unless it is an absolute necessity. Employees who like an independent work environment complement the cat's personality very well.

5 The dog is often called "man's best friend"; likewise, the dog boss is the worker's best friend. These bosses are very extroverted. They love social interaction, and they get along well with everyone in the company. They are happy to help their employees when needed. Finally, they are loyal. They respect their employees, and they treat them well so that they stay working for them.

6 The lion, the bee, the cat, and the dog all have distinct characteristics that distinguish them from one another. These are the four kinds of bosses I have met, but there are certainly more to discover. What is most important is to find the type of boss that matches your own personality to ensure that both of you are happy.

Organizing the Classification Essay

To write a classification essay, divide your topic into related, but different categories. Topics can be categorized in more than one way, but in a classification essay, you must use only one principle or way. For example, teachers can be classified by their personality as *strict*, *friendly*, or *funny*. Another way to classify teachers is by their experience: *expert*, *experienced*, and *inexperienced*. Make sure that you don't include unrelated categories. For instance, you couldn't classify teachers into *strict*, *friendly*, and *inexperienced* because *inexperienced* is a different principle.

The **thesis statement** for a classification essay should state the topic and show that the essay will divide the topic into types or groups.

EXAMPLE

Rentfrow and Gosling's conclusion was that people could be categorized into four distinct musical personalities.

Practice

A. Read the model essay on page 87 again. Complete the missing information in the outline below.

I. Introduction

A. Lead: ______________________________

____

B. Background information: *Most people will have to deal with more than one boss in their lives, and every boss has his or her own personality.*

C. Thesis statement: ______________________________

____

II. Body

A. *The lion* ______________________________

1. *expects employees to follow orders correctly*
2. *has a bad temper*
3. ______________________________

B. ______________________________

1. ______________________________
2. *good role models*
3. *sometimes too busy*

C. ______________________________

1. ______________________________

2. ______________________________

D. *The dog* ______________________________

1. ______________________________

2. ______________________________

3. *happy to help employees when needed*

III. Conclusion

A. Restated thesis: ______________________________

____

B. Final thoughts: *These are the four kinds of bosses I have met, but there are certainly more to discover. What is most important is to find the type of boss that matches your own personality to ensure that both of you are happy.*

B. Each category has one unrelated item. Cross out the item that doesn't belong to the group.

1. Teachers: strict, friendly, ~~female~~, funny
2. Animals: whales, fish, dolphins, penguins
3. Pollution: air, garbage, water, land
4. TV shows: soap opera, comedy, news, drama
5. Social status: unemployed, lower class, middle class, upper class
6. Music: pop, rock, British, classical
7. Weather: snow, rain, water, sleet
8. Art: sculpture, painting, modern, photography

C. ***Look at the professions in the box. Divide them into 3 separate categories and write them in the chart below. Then identify the classification type used for each group.***

accountant	doctor	paramedic
banker	~~firefighter~~	police officer
dentist	nurse	stockbroker

GROUP 1	GROUP 2	GROUP 3
classification type: *people who work in emergency situations*	classification type:	classification type:
1. *firefighter*	1.	1.
2.	2.	2.
3.	3.	3.

WRITING ASSIGNMENT

Write a classification essay. Follow the steps.

STEP 1 **Get ideas.**

A. Choose a topic for your essay. Check (✔) it.

❑ **Topic 1:** Identify and explain three or four different types of students.

❑ **Topic 2:** Identify and explain the different types of friends you have. Try to categorize your friends into three or four different groups.

❑ **Topic 3:** Explain the personalities of different kinds of shoppers.

❑ **Topic 4:** Identify and explain different kinds of love.

B. Brainstorm ideas for your topic using *clustering*. Write your topic in the center of a piece of paper. Use lines to connect ideas that are related to one another.

EXAMPLE

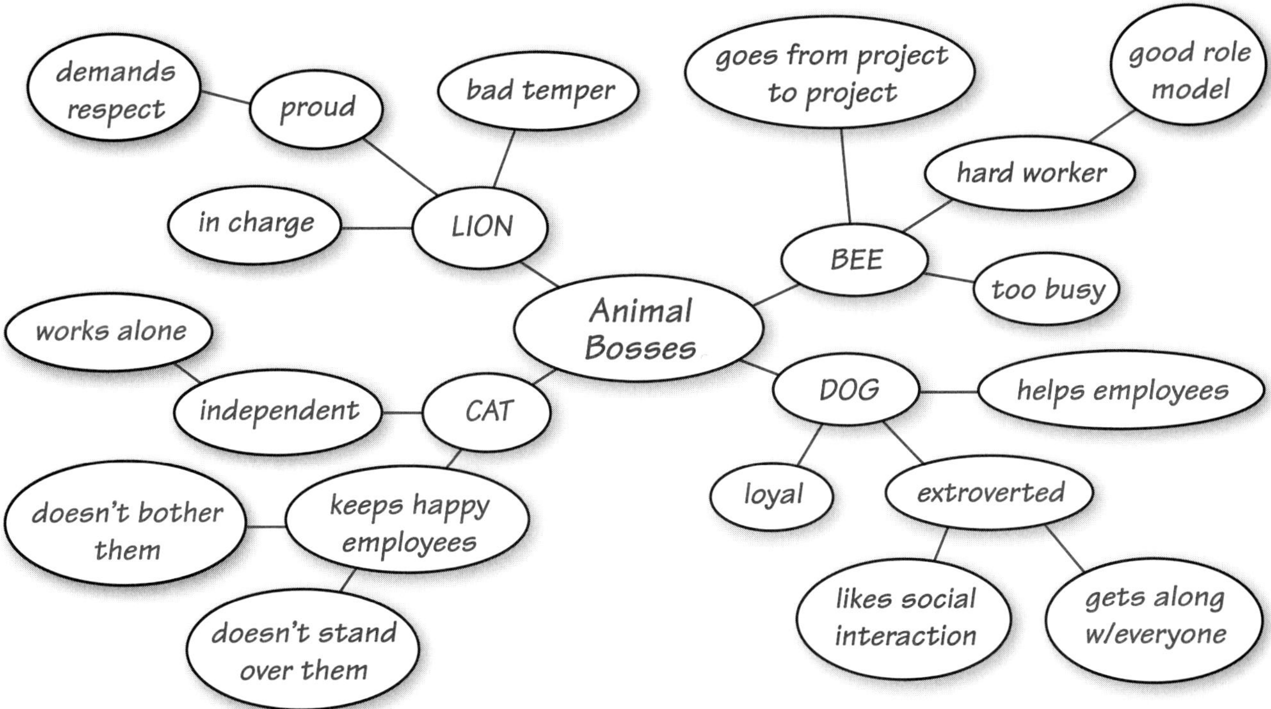

STEP 2 **Organize your ideas.**

Make an outline using the ideas from your clustering map in Step 1.

STEP 3 **Write a rough draft.**

Write your essay. Use your outline from Step 2. Include vocabulary and classification markers from the unit where possible.

STEP 4 **Revise your rough draft.**

Read your essay. Use the Writing Checklist to look for mistakes. Work alone or in pairs.

Writing Checklist

- ❑ Does your introduction have an interesting lead?
- ❑ Does your thesis statement declare the topic and indicate which categories you will write about?
- ❑ Do your body paragraphs use the same principle of classification?
- ❑ Do your body paragraphs include enough supporting information?
- ❑ Does your conclusion end with final thoughts?
- ❑ Did you use classification markers appropriately in your essay?

STEP 5 Edit your writing.

A. Edit your essay. Use the correction symbols chart on page 173. Correct any mistakes in capitalization, punctuation, spelling, verb-tense, or *parallel structure* (words that follow the same grammatical structure).

EXAMPLE

Teachers can be classified as strict, ~~those who are~~ fair, or ~~some teachers are too~~ lenient.

B. Work in pairs. Exchange essays and check each other's work.

STEP 6 Write a final copy.

Correct your mistakes. Copy your final essay and give it to your instructor.

UNIT

6

Gender

Urban

In this unit you will:

- read articles about shopping and fashionable men
- learn to use a Venn diagram to find similarities and differences
- organize and write a comparison-contrast essay

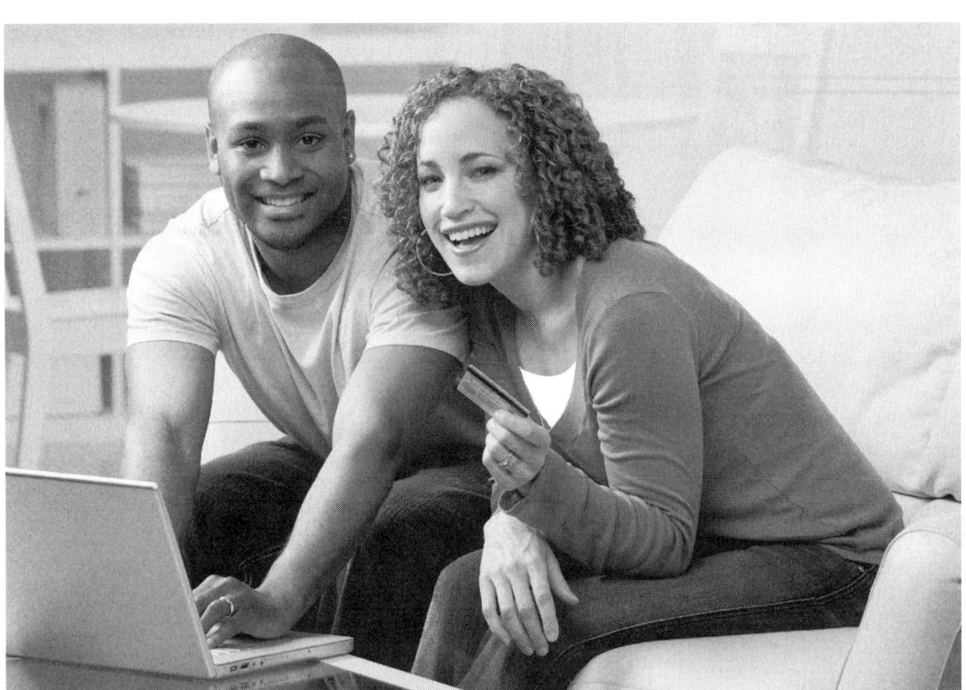

PRE-READING 1

Discussion

Discuss these questions in pairs or small groups.

1. Do you prefer to shop in stores or online?
2. How is online shopping different from traditional store shopping?
3. Who do you think shops more—men or women? Why?

Vocabulary

Read the sentences. Match the boldfaced words with the definitions in the box.

____ 1. Most nurses in America are female. Men **constitute** less than 10 percent of nurses in the United States.

____ 2. My mother looks through the newspaper to find shopping coupons, and then plans her trips to the supermarket **accordingly**.

____ 3. The first MP3 players **emerged** in the late 1990s, but they didn't really become popular until after the turn of the century.

____ 4. Giving women the right to vote was a **remarkable** accomplishment for America. The struggle to change the law took over a hundred years.

____ 5. **Contrary to** what many people believe, some girls like to play video games, and some boys don't enjoy them.

____ 6. Many parents **are inclined to** treat sons and daughters differently because they believe boys and girls think and behave differently.

____ 7. Do you believe that people from the same culture think and act similarly? For example, is there such a thing as an American or Mexican **mentality**?

____ 8. Illiteracy, or not knowing how to read, is a **fundamental** problem which can lead to more complex social and economic problems.

____ 9. Many college students share a **common** goal. They want to earn a degree so that they are able to find a good job.

a. in contrast to b. shared by several people or groups c. combine together to form a particular system, group, result etc. d. in a way that is appropriate for a particular situation or based on what someone has said or done e. a particular type of attitude or way of thinking f. affecting the simplest and most important parts of something g. unusual or surprising and therefore deserving attention or praise h. often do something i. begin to be known or noticed

Shopping by the Sexes

1 A lot can change in 50 years, especially when it comes to men and women. Back in the 1950s, gender roles were more clearly defined: men were the sole breadwinners,[1] and women played the role of "housewife," a job that included everything from cooking to cleaning to taking care of the children. At that time, only one in three women were part of the workforce, and it was men who were supposed to make all of the financial decisions for the family. Today, the situation has changed dramatically, with women now **constituting** about half of all workers. Women have made great progress in their efforts to reach financial equality. Companies have been observing this trend for a while and have changed their marketing **accordingly**, taking advantage of the equal buying power of the modern American woman. Many studies have explored the effects of this equality, and we now have a fascinating look into the different ways men and women approach and think about shopping.

2 Since the Internet **emerged**, shopping has experienced a **remarkable** transformation. Shoppers no longer have to limit themselves to local malls and stores but instead have access to literally millions of online stores from all around the world. Interestingly, American men and women of today both seem to be attracted to the same kinds of products online. Electronics are the hottest items out there; and both men and women shop for cell phones, computers, and digital cameras. However, **contrary to** the popular belief that women enjoy shopping more than men, a number of studies on online shopping have shown that men actually spend more money than women online. They **are** more **inclined to** spend more on a single item than women are. "Women are, in fact, buying more items, but men are buying more expensive things," says Iowa State University professor Tahira K. Hira.

3 The thought process each gender goes through before committing to a purchase also differs. Most men still have a "hunter" approach to shopping, treating it as a mission to be accomplished. They are not as likely as women to bargain shop, which involves checking and comparing prices in different stores in search of the lowest price. They also take bigger risks than women, and this risk-taking **mentality** results in their feeling more comfortable buying products that have only just been put on the shelves. This *it's-new-so-I-want-it* mentality is perhaps one of the reasons men are more likely to spend more on single items than women are.

4 While men are more impulsive,[2] women take a slower and more practical approach to shopping. Marketing studies have shown that women generally do not like to rush into a purchase, and consequently they are not the risk-takers that men tend to be. Another significant difference lies in the practice of bargain shopping. Unlike men, women are bigger and better bargain shoppers, which is

(continued)

[1] **breadwinner:** the member of a family who earns the money to support the others

[2] **impulsive:** tending to do things without thinking about the results, or showing this quality

another reason why they spend less on individual purchases.

5 Being a more patient and thorough[3] shopper is not simply a matter of different shopping habits, say psychologists. It also involves a different way of thinking and behaving. American men are socialized to be more aggressive, goal-oriented,[4] and independent, so they treat shopping as a problem to be solved. This mentality not only explains why they take more risks, but it also explains a **fundamental** difference between the sexes: men prefer shopping alone and don't like asking for help; women, on the other hand, treat shopping as a social activity. Women "talk to get information and to connect [to others]," says psychologist Marilyn A. Sachs. Because they are more relationship-oriented, women prefer to consult with their friends, family, and co-workers before making a purchase, and doing so results in their taking more time to shop and fewer risks when shopping. This contrasts sharply with men, many of whom still believe that asking for help is a sign of weakness.

6 What underlies the differences between male and female shoppers is thus a deeper issue that goes beyond simple statistics on who spends more or who shops more frequently. Although American men and women share a **common** desire to shop, differences exist in the way they think about and approach shopping. But give it 50 more years—who knows what might happen then?

[3] **thorough:** careful to do things correctly, so that you avoid mistakes

[4] **goal-oriented:** making end results a main interest or purpose

Identifying Main Ideas

Read each question. Circle the letter of the best answer.

1. What is the main idea of the reading?
   a. Men and women played very different roles in the 1950s than they do at the present time.
   b. Both men and women like to shop, but approach shopping differently.
   c. Because of the Internet, men and women shop more often and buy the same kinds of products.
   d. Men like to handle problems on their own, whereas women prefer asking others for help.

2. What main point about electronics does the author make in paragraph 2?
   a. Today's electronics include cell phones and digital cameras.
   b. Men and women have a similar desire to buy electronics online.
   c. People can buy electronics both at local stores and on the Internet.
   d. Digital cameras have brought men and women closer together.

3. Which two approaches do men take when they go shopping? Circle two answers.
   a. They like to shop around before committing to a purchase.
   b. They treat shopping as a mission to be accomplished.
   c. They don't mind taking risks when purchasing an item.
   d. They like to compare similar items online and in stores.
4. What is the main idea of paragraph 4?
   a. Men spend more money than women do on online purchases.
   b. Bargain shopping means comparing prices in different stores.
   c. Women don't like to take as many risks as men do.
   d. Women approach shopping in a slow and practical way.
5. According to paragraph 5, which one of the following is *not* true?
   a. Men are socialized to be independent shoppers.
   b. Women treat shopping as a social activity.
   c. Men ask for help from others more than women do.
   d. Women are more relationship-oriented than men are.

Identifying Details

Scan Reading 1. Complete these sentences with the missing information.

1. Women are about ______________ of the American workforce.
2. ______________ are one of the most popular items men and women buy online.
3. Most men still take a "______________" approach to shopping.
4. Women are more likely than men to ______________ shop in order to find the lowest price for an item.

Making Inferences

Infer what the writer would say is true even though it is not directly stated. Check (✔) each statement the writer would agree with.

_____ 1. In the 1950s, husbands and wives did not have equal buying power.

_____ 2. People have beliefs about gender differences that aren't always true.

_____ 3. Men have a harder time dealing with failure than women do.

_____ 4. Shopping comes more naturally to women than it does to men.

_____ 5. American parents teach their sons to value independence.

Using a Venn Diagram

A **Venn diagram** shows similarities and differences between two related topics. Using this diagram can help you to see the comparisons and contrasts a writer makes between two topics.

A Venn diagram consists of two overlapping circles with one circle for each topic. The middle section is for listing similarities between two topics. In the outside sections, you list the unique characteristics that make each topic different from the other.

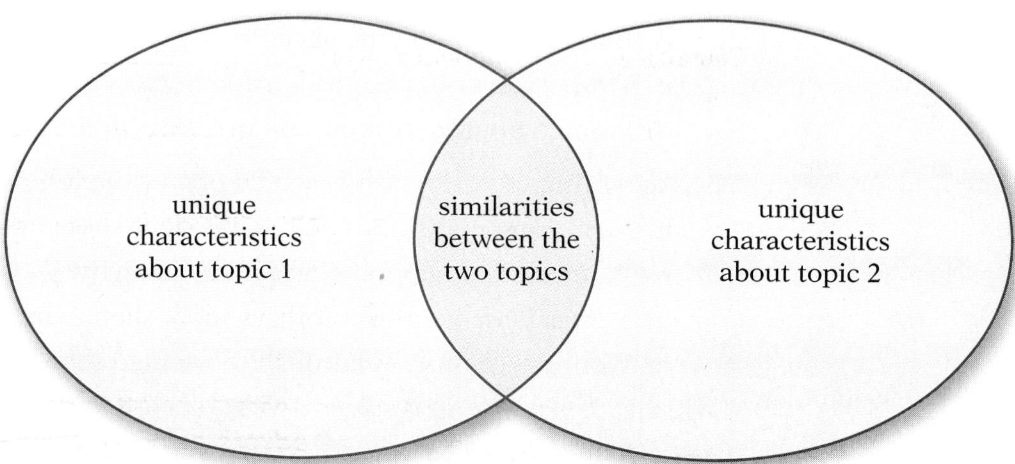

Practice

Scan Reading 1. Complete the Venn diagram below. Add one similarity and three unique characteristics for each topic. Compare your answers in pairs.

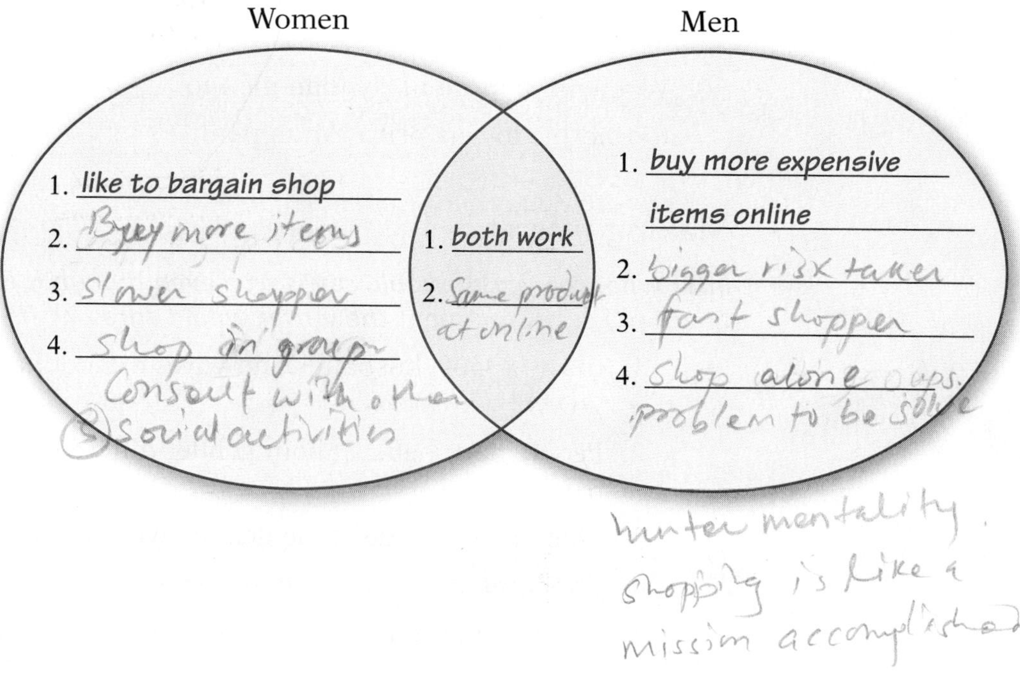

VOCABULARY SKILL

Using Adverb-Adjective Collocations

Many adjectives can become adverbs by adding the suffix *-ly*.

EXAMPLE

ADJECTIVE

John has made <u>remarkable</u> progress in the past two months.

ADVERB

Mr. Jones and Mrs. Gutierrez are <u>remarkably</u> similar in the way they teach.

Certain adverbs collocate (go together) with specific adjectives. For example, the adverb *remarkably* often collocates with the adjectives *similar* and *different* to explain how similar or different two subjects are.

EXAMPLE

Men and woman are <u>remarkably different</u> when it comes to shopping habits.

Practice

This chart lists other adverbs that adjectives often describe. Read each sentence and choose the correct adverb-adjective collocation from the chart.

COMMON ADVERB-ADJECTIVE COLLOCATIONS	
remarkably	similar different
commonly	found known
fundamentally	different wrong
equally	important responsible
widely	available used

1. All children deserve a quality education. Education is ___equally___ ___important___ for boys and girls.
2. Books about gender differences are ____________ ____________. They can be found at bookstores and libraries everywhere.

3. A person who fights for women's freedom and equality in society is commonly known as a "feminist."
4. Many people today believe men and woman should be equally responsible when it comes to raising children.
5. Twins can be remarkably similar in their appearance but very different in their personalities.
6. Most Americans believe that discrimination against someone because of their gender is fundamentaly wrong.

FROM READING TO WRITING

> ***Journal***
> **Choose one of your answers and write a journal entry.**

Reflecting on the Reading

Discuss the questions in pairs or small groups.

1. Do you agree that men treat shopping as a mission, but women treat it as a social activity? Why or why not?
2. According to the reading, men are bigger risk-takers than women. Do you believe this is true? Why or why not?
3. Why do you think men like to purchase items that have just recently been introduced in stores?

PRE-READING 2

Discussion

Discuss the questions in pairs or small groups.

1. Do you think men care less about their appearance than women do? Why or why not?
2. Is it important for men to spend time on their looks? Explain.

Vocabulary

Read the sentences. Match the boldfaced words with the definitions in the box.

____ 1. Psychologists have been observing the growing **phenomenon** of stay-at-home-dads, or men who don't work so they can raise their children.

____ 2. Gender **comprises** your gender identity, or how you feel about being male or female, and your gender expression, or how you show it.

____ 3. There are **various** ways for people to control how others see them, from the words they use, to the clothes they wear, to the type of car they drive.

____ 4. In very multicultural cities, different **versions** of newspapers and magazines exist for people who speak different native languages.

____ 5. A common **stereotype** is that girls are more emotional than boys. However, some childhood experts argue that this idea is not true.

____ 6. It is easy to make **assumptions** about other cultures, but until you live in the culture, it is difficult to say which beliefs are true and which are not.

____ 7. Spending time in another country may make people more **liberal**, since they get to know cultures that are different from the one they grew up in.

____ 8. As children **interact with** their environment, they develop a better understanding of how the world affects them and how they can affect others.

a. consist of particular parts, groups, etc.
b. have an effect on each other
c. willing to understand or respect the different behavior or ideas of other people
d. an idea, usually shared by many people, of what a particular group of people is like, especially one that is wrong or unfair
e. something that you think is true although you have no proof
f. several different
g. something that happens or exists in society, science, or nature that is often discussed or studied
h. a copy or form of something that is slightly different from other forms of it

READING 2

Fashionable Men

1 Researchers have made an interesting discovery about modern-day men—they spend a lot of time and money on their appearance. Today, global sales of male grooming products bring in billions of dollars a year, and the industry is not expected to slow down. Is this a sign that the modern man is becoming increasingly concerned about his appearance? Some people might think that fashion-conscious[1] men are a new **phenomenon**, but a look through history reveals that men have actually been concerned about their looks for thousands of years.

2 The first documented cases of fashionable men occurred around 10,000 BCE in ancient Egypt. The Egyptians stressed the importance of good hygiene and health. Men applied oils and creams to their skin to protect themselves from the hot sun and dry winds of the desert. In addition to the perfumes they wore, men also had their own makeup boxes that **comprised** special jars of colored makeup which they applied to their eyes, lips, cheeks, and nails. All of this was done not to impress others but rather to keep their ancient gods happy.

3 The ancient Greeks also valued male health and beauty, but in contrast to the Egyptians, the Greeks' use of cosmetics was for purely aesthetic[2] reasons. Greek men applied flower-based oils to their skin and quickly adopted Egyptian oils after the Greek king Alexander the Great took over Egypt in 332 BCE. Alexander was the man responsible for making the use of oils common practice in daily Greek life. During his conquests,[3] he would take plant cuttings and send them to Athens, where they were grown and made into perfumes and **various** skin oils for men to use before and after bathing. Alexander felt so strongly about cosmetics that when he defeated King Darius of Persia, he even threw away the king's makeup box of ointments and perfumes as a symbol of victory.

4 Around 100 AD, the Romans took men's grooming products to a whole new level. Like the Greeks, Roman men used skin oils before and after bathing, but they were also passionate about the beauty of their face and hair. They used a combination of sheep's fat and blood on their fingernails for nail polish and frequently dyed their hair blond to make themselves appear younger. They had their own **versions** of eye shadow, blush for the cheeks, and powder for whitening the face. For the Romans, it seems nothing was off limits[4] in their search to make men more attractive. Vanity[5] did not have a negative connotation,[6] but instead was viewed as a natural consequence of health and beauty.

5 In 16th-century England, the emphasis on male beauty was directly tied to financial status. Rich English men would use face-whitening powder because they believed a pale face was a sign of wealth. Keeping their

[1] **fashion-conscious:** thinking a lot about fashion
[2] **aesthetic:** relating to beauty and the study of beauty

[3] **conquest:** the act of defeating an army or taking land by fighting
[4] **be off limits:** be unacceptable to do
[5] **vanity:** too much pride in yourself, so that you are always thinking about yourself and your appearance
[6] **connotation:** a feeling or an idea that a word makes you think of

skin healthy was an elaborate procedure that consisted of bathing in wine, applying oils to the skin, and using an egg and honey mask on the face to hide wrinkles. On formal occasions, men further enhanced their appearance by using lipstick, bleaching their hair, and wearing wigs.

6 Men today, and especially young men, are equally concerned about their appearance and body image, and this trend is not necessarily culture-specific. In 2006, American men spent $4.8 million on male grooming products; in parts of Asia, the male cosmetic industry is just as strong, if not stronger. "Asian men increasingly want to look after their looks and are prepared to spend to do so," says marketing researcher Carol Sarthou of the Phillipines. The Chinese even have a name for these kinds of men: *aimei nanren*, which translates to "love beauty men." Such men are rejecting the modern-day "masculine" **stereotype**, which says that men aren't supposed to care about their appearance. In today's world, that **assumption** is simply not true. Modern-day society is becoming more **liberal**, and no longer expects all men to fit one definition of "masculinity."

7 It is often said that history repeats itself—trends come and go as people's beliefs and values change over time and cultures **interact with** one another. Modern man's interest in grooming and cosmetic products is not a new phenomenon. The eye creams, facial masks, and moisturizers that men are buying today are simply different versions of the same idea, one that began 12,000 years ago. The history of fashionable men shows that the more things change, the more they stay the same.

Identifying Main Ideas

Match the two parts of each sentence.

b 1. Egyptian men . . .

a 2. Ancient Greek men . . .

e 3. Ancient Roman men . . .

d 4. 16th-century English men . . .

c 5. Modern men . . .

a. began using grooming products because of Alexander the Great.
b. used beauty products to please their ancient gods.
c. reject the stereotype that men aren't supposed to care about how they look.
d. believed that looking good meant that you were rich.
e. thought that it was natural for men to use beauty products.

Identifying Details

Complete the chart by listing two to three examples for each culture.

	HEALTH AND BEAUTY PRODUCTS
ANCIENT EGYPTIANS	makeup boxes; oils and creams; perfumes
ANCIENT GREEKS	flower-based oils, perfums, skin oils.
ANCIENT ROMANS	sheeps fat and blood, powder
16TH-CENTURY ENGLISH MEN	whitening powder, egg and honey mask

Making Inferences

Infer what the writer would say is true even though it is not directly stated. Check (✔) each statement the writer would agree with.

____ 1. Ancient Egyptian men used more beauty products than women did.

✓ 2. Greek King Alexander the Great was a powerful ruler.

✓ 3. The Ancient Romans considered young people more beautiful than older people.

____ 4. Asian men buy more grooming products than American men do.

✓ 5. People today have different opinions on what "masculinity" means.

FROM READING TO WRITING

Journal
Choose one of your answers and write a journal entry.

Reflecting on the Reading

Discuss the questions in pairs or small groups.

1. Does modern-day society place too much importance on physical beauty?
2. For men, what are the advantages and disadvantages of using cosmetics? Would you want your son to use them?

The Comparison-Contrast Essay

> ***Vocabulary***
> For more practice with vocabulary, go to pages 184–185.

Comparison essays compare two or more topics by discussing their similarities or both their similarities *and* differences. Reading 2 was a historical comparison that discussed the similarities and differences between fashionable men at different moments in history. **Contrast essays** focus primarily on the differences between two topics. Reading 1, for example, compared how and why American men and women shop differently. Contrast essays are a very common assignment in college courses. They might ask students to explore the differences between two ideas, principles, people, or periods in history.

Read the model essay.

MODEL

Girls, Boys, and Toys

1 Like most ten-year-old American boys, Jacob Ryan loves video games. His sister, Jessica, is much more interested in her doll collection. Do Jacob and Jessica represent most boys and girls? Certainly, boys and girls can and do share common interests. However, toy companies are gender-biased. They make different products and market their products differently according to male and female stereotypes.

2 The toys that companies make for boys differ remarkably from those for girls. Companies assume that boys are active and aggressive. No toy illustrates this stereotype better than the action figure. Most action figures are muscular and designed to be used in imaginative adventures. Some are intended to engage in make-believe fights against one another. Furthermore, many are given violent jobs like crime fighters and wrestlers. The message from these toys is clear. If you are a boy, you love action and conflict. Unlike boys' toys, girls' toys reflect the assumption that girls are more passive, creative, and friendly. Popular toys include jewelry-making and dress-up kits, and of course, dolls. Barbie™ is still the leader in the doll industry. Barbie is a lover of fashion and shopping, which are stereotypical female interests. Furthermore, instead of enemies, the Barbie collection offers various doll friends. The message is that girls are more "naturally" relationship-oriented than boys.

(continued)

3 The way companies market their toys to boys and girls also differs. Toy commercials directed towards boys are often loud and fast-paced. Many toy commercials portray boys misbehaving or doing violent things, such as crashing toy cars together. Some researchers have also noted that toy advertisements tend to show boys in fantasy situations. The underlying message is that boys are aggressive, independent, and creative. Advertisements for girls follow a very different theme, portraying them as gentle and calm. Unlike boys, girls are most often shown playing in the home, often with dolls or stuffed animals. Most of the time, the girls are well-behaved. In all, toy companies are inclined to treat girls as passive individuals who enjoy domestic life and don't cause any trouble.

4 Even though men and women have changed, toy companies continue to hold onto old gender stereotypes; accordingly, the industry tells boys to be active and antisocial but expects girls to be passive and socially acceptable. Children are easily influenced. Consequently, parents need to talk to their sons and daughters about these stereotypical images. After all, parents should have a bigger influence on their children than toy companies do, right?

Practice

Answer the questions.

1. Does this essay examine similarities, differences, or both similarities and differences?
2. Which gender is always discussed first?
3. What do toy companies assume about boys and girls?
4. What are the writer's final thoughts on the topic?

Organizing the Comparison-Contrast Essay

Comparison-contrast essays can compare many topics, but most compare only two. Whether you focus on similarities or differences, the two topics must have something in common. For example, you cannot compare life in Los Angeles with life in Japan because one is a city and the other is a country. Instead, you need to choose the same level of comparison, such as comparing life in two cities like Los Angeles and Tokyo.

Thesis Statement The thesis statement for a comparison essay should state the topic and identify whether the focus is on similarities, differences, or both. The thesis statement for a contrast essay should state the topic and indicate that the focus is on differences.

EXAMPLES

Both men and women like to shop, but they approach shopping in different ways.

Toy companies make different products and market their products differently according to male and female stereotypes.

Point-by-Point Organization Many comparison-contrast essays follow a point-by-point organization. For shorter essays, each specific similarity or difference between the two topics is discussed in its own body paragraph. The writer presents the first point of comparison between the topics, and then the second, the third, and so on. Typically, the topics are always presented in the same order in every body paragraph.

EXAMPLE

Thesis statement: Toy companies make different products and market their products differently according to common stereotypes of girls and boys.

I. Toys (point of comparison 1)
   - A. Boys
   - B. Girls

II. Advertising (point of comparison 2)
   - A. Boys
   - B. Girls

Practice

A. ***Are these pairs of topics on the same level of comparison? Mark the topics* C *(comparable) or* NC *(not comparable). If they are not comparable, change one in each pair so they have the same level of comparison.***

dining in a restaurant

_NC_ 1. ~~fast food restaurants~~ / dining at home

_C_ 2. frozen food / fresh food

___ 3. living with family / living alone

___ 4. holidays in Japan / New Year's Eve

___ 5. clubs in New York City / clubs in Los Angeles

___ 6. life before computers / the Internet

___ 7. chatting online / shopping online

___ 8. CD players / MP3 players

B. Read the thesis statements. Add one or two points of comparison for each statement.

1. Men and women have different styles of communication.
   a. with friends
   b. at work
   c. at home
2. Today's jobs require more computer skills than they did in the past.
   a. architects
   b. journalists
   c. doctors
3. Urban and suburban living differ in three significant ways.
   a. cost
   b. pollution
   c. traffic
4. Doing research online differs from doing traditional library research.
   a. convenience
   b. Fast
   c. many information
5. Teenagers have many different clothing styles to choose from nowadays.
   a. ______________
   b. ______________
   c. ______________

Using Comparison and Contrast Markers

To make their comparisons clear, writers use a variety of comparison and contrast markers in their essays:

COMPARISON MARKERS (SIMILARITIES)	CONTRAST MARKERS (DIFFERENCES)
Like + (noun) *Similar to* + (noun) **EXAMPLE** Like women, men also like to shop.	*Unlike* + (noun) *In contrast to* + (noun) *Unlike* + (noun) **EXAMPLE** Unlike men, women often ask friends for shopping advice.
Just as + (subject + verb), (subject + verb) *Both* (subject) *and* (subject) + (verb) **EXAMPLE** Both men and women like to shop.	*While* + (subject + verb), (subject + verb) *Although* + (subject + verb), (subject + verb) *Whereas* + (subject + verb), (subject + verb) **EXAMPLE** While women often ask friends for shopping advice, men prefer shopping alone.
(subject + verb); *similarly*, (subject + verb) **EXAMPLE** Women enjoy shopping online; similarly, men spend more online than at the mall.	(subject + verb); *however*, (subject + verb) (subject + verb); *on the other hand*, (subject + verb) **EXAMPLE** Women often ask friends for shopping advice; on the other hand, men prefer shopping independently.

Practice

Combine the two sentences using the comparison-contrast markers in parentheses. Use correct punctuation.

1. New York has an exciting nightlife. Tokyo has an exciting nightlife.
   a. (*like*) Like New York, Tokyo has an exciting nightlife.
   b. (*both . . . and*) Both New York and Tokyo have an exciting nightlife

2. Children learn about gender from their parents. They learn gender norms from school.

   a. (*similarly*) ______________________________

   b. (*just as*) ______________________________

3. Debby is a social person. Her brother is more introverted.

   a. (*while*) ______________________________

   b. (*in contrast*) ______________________________

4. Men are aggressive. Women are less aggressive.

   a. (*in contrast to*) ______________________________

   b. (*however*) ______________________________

WRITING ASSIGNMENT

Write a comparison-contrast essay. Follow the steps.

STEP 1 Get ideas.

A. Choose a topic for your essay. Check (✔) it.

❑ **Topic 1:** Compare two people in your family of the same gender but of different generations, such as a mother and daughter.

❑ **Topic 2:** Compare how mothers and fathers raise their children. Do they take similar and/or different approaches?

❑ **Topic 3:** Compare women today with women of the past. How have women changed in the last 50 years?

❑ **Topic 4:** Look at newspaper and magazine ads directed at women and ads directed at men. Compare and contrast the messages each sends about gender.

B. Make a Venn diagram on a separate piece of paper to list the similarities and differences between the subjects of your topic. Focus on similarities, differences, or both similarities and differences.

STEP 2 Organize your ideas.

Make an outline for your essay. Choose two or three points from your diagram in Step 1.

STEP 3 Write a rough draft.

Write your essay. Use your outline from Step 2. Include vocabulary from the unit where possible.

STEP 4 **Revise your rough draft.**

Read your essay. Use the Writing Checklist to look for mistakes. Work alone or in pairs.

Writing Checklist

- ❑ Does your introduction have a clear thesis statement that focuses on similarities, differences, or both?
- ❑ Does each body paragraph focus on only one point of comparison?
- ❑ Does each body paragraph present the topics in the same order?
- ❑ Does your conclusion have a restated thesis?
- ❑ Did you include comparison-contrast markers appropriately in your essay?

STEP 5 **Edit your writing.**

A. Edit your essay. Use the correction symbols on page 173. Correct any mistakes in capitalization, punctuation, spelling, verb-tense, or word form, such as comparative adjective and adverb mistakes.

EXAMPLES

COMPARATIVE ADJECTIVE

Shopping online is ~~more~~ quicker than shopping in stores.

COMPARATIVE ADVERB

more slowly

Women shop ~~slower~~ than men do.

B. Work in pairs. Exchange essays and check each other's work.

STEP 6 **Write a final copy.**

Correct your mistakes. Copy your final essay and give it to your instructor.

UNIT

7

Human Nature

In this unit you will:

- read articles about fear and laughter
- learn to recognize a causal chain
- organize and write a cause-effect essay

PRE-READING 1

Discussion

Discuss the questions in pairs or small groups.

1. Look at the picture. Why do people like to watch horror movies?
2. What kinds of movies do you enjoy watching? Why?

Vocabulary

Read the article. Match each boldfaced word or phrase with the definition in the box. Write the letter.

The Human Brain

The human brain is an amazing organ. Through time, it has **evolved** (1____) into the most complex brain found on earth. The brain contains billions of neurons, or nerve cells, whose **role** (2____) is to transmit information to other cells in the body. Feeling pain, for example, **activates** (3____) cells in the brain to tell you that you are in danger. The brain is responsible for all feelings, whether it be a **sense** (4____) of fear or relief. As humans, we have an **innate** (5____) capacity to feel emotions, which explains why newborn babies naturally cry when they are upset.

Neurons in the brain help us think and remember information. When we learn new information, the neurons **undergo** (6____) a process whereby they make connections with other neurons. Making these **bonds** (7____) involves several different **phases** (8____), but in total they take less than a second from beginning to end. When the process is finished, a memory begins to form. Certain memories, like knowing how to drive a car, are actually **subconscious** (9____); they are automatic, and we don't have to think about them. In contrast, thinking about how to get from one place to another is a **conscious** (10____) process because it requires active thought.

a. experience an event, a change, etc.
b. hidden from awareness
c. a feeling about something
d. the way in which someone or something is involved in an activity or situation
e. of a process of development or change
f. something that unites two or more things, people, or groups
g. part of a person's character from the time they are born
h. aware of what is happening
i. develop by gradually changing
j. make something start working

READING 1

Why You Can't Turn Away

By Richard Coniff

1 Like most of us, you have probably spent too many hours captivated by television images of people suffering through all our worst nightmares: You might have seen them fleeing a deadly tide,[1] stumbling out of bombed subway tunnels, or walking past the destruction of a hurricane in the streets of a great American city. And after that first it-can't-happen-here moment of horror, you probably also experienced a confusing flood of other emotions. One moment you're crying along with a father who's lost everything; the next moment you turn away with contempt[2] toward the victims, or in embarrassment over your own voyeuristic[3] curiosity. Why do we watch? Why do we grow so emotional about people we'll never meet? Why do we sit through endless replays of the same horrible scenes (as if maybe this time they'll come out differently)? And why do men in particular have to joke about it afterward?

2 Scientists say we watch partly for self-preservation: Paying attention to other people's disasters is a way to keep the same things from happening to us. That's one reason we like thrillers and shark-attack movies so much. It may seem shocking to associate the experience of a hurricane with watching a horror movie. But scary reality and scary fantasy both affect biological systems that **have evolved** to help us save our own lives.

3 Psychologists call it *instructed fear*, and the explanation starts with the victims themselves. Let's say you narrowly escaped the flooding of a hurricane. "Flashbulb memories" of the event are probably imprinted on your brain,[4] particularly in the amygdala, which is your **subconscious** fear center. If you then encounter some hint of that experience—a cloud formation, a change in the wind—the amygdala's **role** is to put you on alert before your **conscious** mind suspects that anything is wrong. That way, you have a head start on your escape route and a better chance of getting out alive.

4 What's more surprising is that almost the same response occurs even in people who only saw the devastation on television. "When you watch somebody else in a fear-learning circumstance," says New York University neuroscientist Elizabeth Phelps, Ph.D., "you will have a reaction in the amygdala as if it were happening to you." When you pass a bad accident on the highway, you feel the fear that the victims felt, and it helps prepare your own subconscious first-alert system in case you ever face a similar crisis.

5 But our intense interest in disasters isn't just a matter of self-preservation. We're also built to connect with other people and share their emotions. When someone looks frightened, our eyebrows also rise in fear, often without our being aware of it. When we see a child's face in anguish,[5] we make the

[1] **tide:** the regular rising and lowering of the level of the ocean
[2] **contempt:** a feeling that someone or something is not important or deserves no respect
[3] **voyeuristic:** enjoying watching other people's private behavior or suffering
[4] **be imprinted on your brain:** If something is imprinted on your brain, you can never forget it.
[5] **anguish:** mental or physical suffering caused by extreme worry or pain

same face, and doing so actually causes us to feel sorry, too. When we see someone else in pain, it **activates** the pain-sensitive regions of our own brains. This kind of "emotional contagion"[6] happens not just during disasters, but anytime we're with other people: You smile at me, I smile back. It's part of our human nature. Our brains are actually equipped with "mirror neurons" to help us mimic[7] the people around us. Why?

6 "We are very much social creatures," says J. Philippe Rushton, Ph.D., a psychologist at the University of Western Ontario, "and empathy is part of the genetic glue that binds us to other people." Being on the same emotional page helped keep families and tribes together during our evolution, when food was limited and predators were abundant. Groups that didn't "click" tended to **undergo** a brief, bloody lesson in natural selection.[8] As a result, empathy, emotional contagion, mirror neurons, and other mechanisms for social bonding are now built into our biology.

7 Television simply "grafts onto[9] these **innate** systems," says Rushton, "and when we look at people suffering 12,000 miles away, our bodies react in the same way." Here's the problem: Our long evolutionary history of group living has caused us to feel a **bond** with people who are, one way or another, close to us. Then television brings the whole world into our living rooms, as if people at the other end of the earth were actually our neighbors.

8 What about our appetite for seeing the same horrific images over and over—then joking about them afterward? Both behaviors are attempts to take away the terrible sting from almost unthinkable events. "We keep going back to it," says UCLA psychiatrist Mark Thompson, M.D. "We don't want to, but we keep going back, saying, 'Oh my gosh, it's terrible.' And part of it is about mastering this **sense** of helplessness. You see it, you see it, you see it, and then it becomes less frightening." It's like teenagers going through a **phase** of addiction to horror movies. Then suddenly they master their fears and put the fascination behind them.

9 And the jokes? They're one way we begin to heal. In the immediate aftermath of a disaster, we practice what Pennsylvania State University folklorist Bill Ellis, Ph.D., calls "strategic suppression[10] of humor." The sense of threat and injury is still too strong. Then the jokes start to come, focused at first on denial, anger, and the need to assign blame. The second wave of jokes, says Ellis, typically uses gross humor[11] to gain distance from the painful realities of death and injury. That's sick, right? On the contrary, says Ellis, it's how we come to terms with the unthinkable, "and the fact that it's done in an unexpected way makes it a triumph of the human imagination over reality." We turn away from the pain and go back to our daily business. A joke reminds us that life is, after all, still worth living.

---

[6] **contagion:** a feeling or attitude that spreads quickly
[7] **mimic:** copy the way someone speaks or behaves
[8] **natural selection:** the process by which only plants and animals that are naturally appropriate for life in their environment will continue to live, while all others will die
[9] **graft onto:** join together with

[10] **suppression:** the act of stopping yourself from showing your feelings or from doing an action
[11] **gross humor:** rude, sick, or violent joking that can be offensive to others

Identifying Main Ideas

Scan Reading 1. Then mark the statements* M *(main idea) or* S *(supporting idea).

____ 1. Watching disasters can help people avoid or survive similar situations in the future.

____ 2. When you see a car accident, your amygdala makes you feel the fear of the victims.

____ 3. Experiencing and watching danger both have the same effect on the brain.

____ 4. Feeling a change in the wind could remind someone of the experience of a hurricane.

____ 5. It is normal for people to smile back at someone who is smiling at them.

____ 6. We keep watching horrible scenes on TV to make them seem less frightening.

____ 7. People joke about disasters because it helps them deal with the pain of seeing them.

Identifying Details

Match the words with their definitions.

____ 1. amygdala

____ 2. emotional contagion

____ 3. mirror neurons

____ 4. strategic suppression of humor

____ 5. flashbulb memories

a. feeling what other people feel

b. brain cells that make us mimic other people

c. the brain's subconscious fear center

d. not making jokes immediately following a horrible event

e. images in the brain of specific experiences from our past

Making Inferences

Infer what the writer would say is true even though it is not directly stated. Check (✔) each statement the writer would agree with.

____ 1. Most people don't understand why they want to see disasters.

____ 2. The amygdala doesn't distinguish real events from fictional events.

____ 3. Humans were more scared in the past than they are now.

____ 4. Most teenagers become addicted to watching horror movies.

____ 5. Social creatures are more likely to survive than unsocial ones.

____ 6. Watching too much violence on TV can be dangerous.

____ 7. Men joke about disasters more than women do.

Recognizing a Causal Chain

READING SKILL

Writers often discuss causes and effects together. Sometimes a cause leads to an effect, which leads to another cause, which leads to an additional effect, and so on. This series of causes and effects is called a **causal chain**.

When identifying causal chains, remember that effects change into causes of other effects. In the causal chain below, each effect becomes a cause. For example, doing poorly in school may be an *effect* of not doing homework, but it could also be a *cause* of making a student's parents upset.

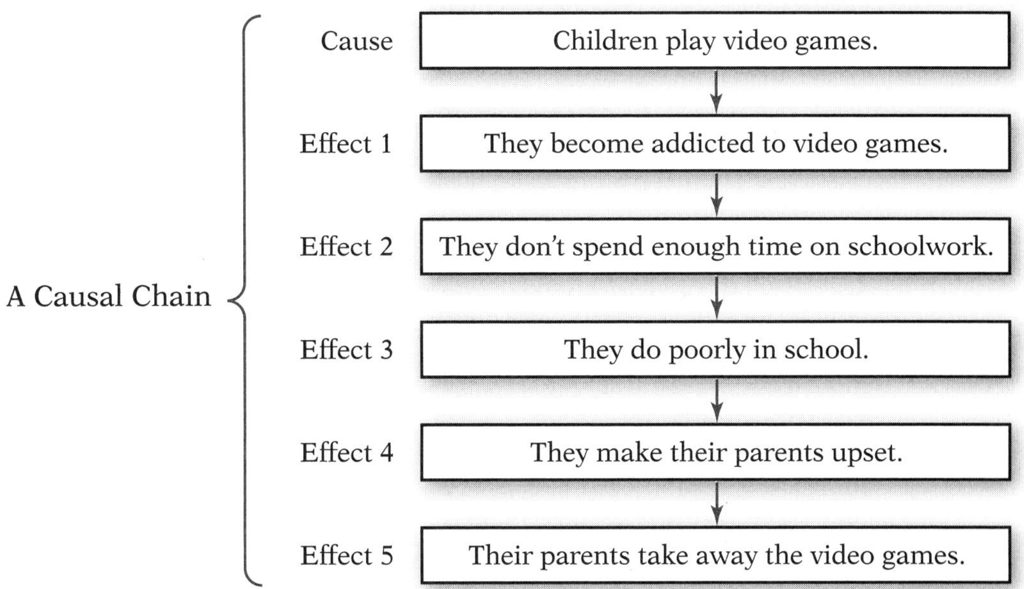
A Causal Chain
Cause
Children play video games.
Effect 1
They become addicted to video games.
Effect 2
They don't spend enough time on schoolwork.
Effect 3
They do poorly in school.
Effect 4
They make their parents upset.
Effect 5
Their parents take away the video games.

Practice

A. Scan paragraph 3 of Reading 1. Number the sentences in the correct order to complete the causal chain.

____ 1. Your chances of survival increase.

_1_ 2. You narrowly escape the flooding of a hurricane.

____ 3. The amygdala puts you on alert when you encounter a similar experience.

____ 4. You have a head start on your escape route.

____ 5. Flashbulb memories of the event are imprinted in the amygdala.

B. Think about the possible effects of moving to a foreign country. Create a causal chain. Share your causal chains in pairs.

VOCABULARY SKILL

Understanding Latin Prefixes

A **prefix** is a group of letters that, when added to the beginning of certain words, change their meaning. Many English prefixes come from Latin, and some have the meaning of prepositions. For instance, the prefix *sub-* acts like the preposition "under." *Sub-* can be put on the word *conscious* to form a new word *subconscious*, or "under conscious," which is close to the dictionary definition of being "under," or hidden from, your awareness.

Look at the chart of some common English prefixes and their meanings.

PREFIX	MEANING
sub-	under
inter-	between
in-	in, into
pre-	before

Practice

A. Add a prefix to each boldfaced word to create the definition that follows.

1. __sub__**side:** gradually go down or decrease
2. __in__**take:** the amount of food, fuel, etc., that is eaten by someone or put into something
3. __inter__**racial:** between different races of people
4. __Sub__**ordinate:** less important than something else, or in a lower position with less authority
5. __pre__**mature:** happening before the natural or appropriate time
6. __in__**put:** ideas, advice, money, or effort that you put into a job, meeting, etc.
7. __inter__**cultural:** between or involving two or more countries or societies
8. __pre__**existing:** existing before something else

B. Complete the sentences with words from Exercise A.

1. Inter racial marriages in the United States mostly involve couples whose ancestors are from Europe, Africa, Latin America, or Asia.
2. The company president asked his supervisors for their in put at the annual meeting.
3. The average person's daily food in take should be between 2,000 and 3,000 calories.
4. Although the number of pre mature births has increased in the United States, most young babies can be saved today thanks to modern medicine.
5. The flu causes a high fever and body aches, but these effects usually sub side within a week.
6. In any company, a vice president is Sub ordinate to a president.

FROM READING TO WRITING

Journal
Choose one of your answers and write a journal entry.

Reflecting on the Reading

Discuss the questions in pairs or small groups.

1. Do you agree with the author of Reading 1 that watching disasters is natural and normal? Explain.
2. People deal with painful situations in different ways. Making jokes is one way. What are other ways people handle difficult experiences in life?
3. How important is the support of family and friends to you? Is it more important during difficult times? Explain.

PRE-READING 2

Discussion

Discuss the questions in pairs or small groups.

1. How many times do you think you laugh a day? What in life makes you laugh?
2. What is the difference between laughing *with* someone and laughing *at* someone?

Vocabulary

Read the boldfaced words and their definitions. Then complete each sentence with the correct word or phrase. Change the form of words as needed.

assure:	tell someone that something will definitely happen or is definitely true, so that he or she is less worried
attribute (something) **to:**	say that a situation, state, or event is caused by something
collaboratively:	characterized by working together with someone or something in order to achieve something
facilitate:	make easier
no matter:	without being affected by different situations or problems
promote:	help something to develop and be successful
stem from:	develop as a result of something else
ultimately:	in the end; eventually

1. The project couldn't be done by one person, so the workers worked ____________ to finish it.
2. Many colleges offer festivals on campus in order to ____________ a feeling of community among the students.
3. Doctors ____________ long life ____________ a number of different factors, including eating well, being physically active, and having a healthy family history.
4. Chat rooms ____________ fast and easy communication between people in different parts of the world.
5. Linda knew she had a lot of work to do, but she ____________ her boss that she wouldn't leave until it was all finished.
6. Psychologists believe gossiping, or talking about other people, ____________ people's need to make social comparisons between themselves and others.
7. Joseph is determined to become a doctor ____________ how long it takes or how much it costs.
8. Today's robots can perform many tasks that they are instructed to do, but scientists hope they will ____________ be able to think for themselves.

READING 2

To Laugh Is Human

What did the sea say to the seashore? Nothing, it just waved.

1 Did you find this joke funny? Why or why not? Most of us don't know why we laugh at some jokes and not at others. Even to scientists, laughter is still quite a mystery. What they do know is that our ability to laugh is innate. Babies begin to laugh at three to four months of age, well before they produce their first words, suggesting that the brain is biologically programmed[1] to make us laugh from the time we are born. Though laughter seems so simple, scientists have also discovered that producing laughter involves a very complex process that requires many parts of the brain to work **collaboratively**. We have no control over this process because laughter is not conscious, but rather an automatic response that comes from the mind. What is still unclear to scientists, however, is *why* we laugh, and what some have learned so far is that most laughter is not the result of hearing a great joke. In fact, they think that laughter actually **stems from** our basic human need to feel close to one another, and that this evolved from an even more basic need to survive.

2 Dr. Robert Provine, who wrote an article on laughter in the journal *American Scientist*, believes humans laugh primarily because it serves as a kind of "social glue" that keeps people connected to one another. We laugh with others because it makes us feel a bond with them, and that bond in turn gives us a sense of trust and comfort. To Provine, laughter is an unconscious reaction that has evolved to help us know who our true friends are. **No matter** how hard we try, we are unable to make ourselves laugh; consequently, when we laugh, others can be certain that it is an honest reaction, and honesty is key when building and maintaining friendships.

3 Provine bases his theory on his own observations of people in traditional social settings, such as coffee shops and malls. In listening in on over twelve hundred conversations between people, Provine found that "most conversational laughter is not a response to structured attempts at humor, such as jokes or stories." In fact, less than 20 percent of the laughter he witnessed was the result of humor. Instead, he found that most laughter, between 80 and 90 percent, actually came after extremely common remarks like, "Look, it's Andre," or "I'll see you guys later." These remarks may not seem terribly funny, but that isn't the point, says Provine. Laughing at others' remarks simply acts as a friendly social signal, telling them that we feel a connection with them.

4 Since laughter is seen as a social cue[2] that we send to others, it can also help explain why it is so contagious. Studies have proven that when people see or hear something funny, they are 30 times more likely to laugh when they are with others than when they are alone; scientists **attribute** this

(continued)

[1] **biologically programmed:** made to happen by our genes

[2] **cue:** an action or event that is a signal for something else to happen

to a fear we all have of being singled out[3] from a group. Wanting to be accepted by others is part of human nature. Nobody wants to feel left out, and mirroring other people's laughter is a way to signal to others that you feel the way they do, which makes us feel more bonded to one another. The brain realized this a long time ago, and group laughter has occurred ever since.

5 Humans have not always laughed just so they can feel closer to others, however. Anthropologists point out that this social function of laughter was born out of[4] an even more fundamental human need. Laughter, they believe, came about because it contributed to our very survival as a species. Anthropologists hypothesize that sharing laughter ensured our ancestors a higher survival rate because it **facilitated** greater cooperation between individuals. Life back then was a numbers game, and there was power in numbers. Those who were able to cooperate with one another and work as a group were more successful at finding food and fighting off enemies. Humans learned quickly that greater cooperation led to survival, and the brain in turn realized that laughing with others increased our chances of finding people to cooperate, hunt, eat, live, and **ultimately**, survive with.

6 Even tickling seems to have stemmed from our need to survive. Researcher Jaak Panksepp and Dr. Provine believe that humans were able to laugh before they were able to speak, or in other words, that laughter was one of our earliest forms of verbal communication. They suspect that the first human laughter came from being tickled, which was important during a time when we were unable to tell others whether our touching of another person was friendly or aggressive. "Primal[5] laughter evolved as a signaling device[6] to highlight readiness for friendly interaction," says Panksepp. Laughing when being tickled **assured** others, such as our close friends and family, that it was playful touching rather than dangerous fighting. Without this signal, humans would have misunderstood what was happening, which could have led to some very disastrous consequences.

7 Because laughter was such an effective communication tool for survival, it has remained alongside language as part of our human nature. The human brain wants us to laugh because it has learned through many years of experience that sharing laughs with others **promotes** both bonding and security. We used to laugh with others in order to help us stay alive, but today laughter has evolved into a way to keep better connected with one another. With all this being said, however, there might be an even more fundamental reason behind our need to laugh, and one that doesn't require elaborate explanations. That is, when it really comes down to it, maybe laughing just feels good.

[3] **single out:** choose someone or something from among a group of similar people or things, especially in order to praise them or criticize them

[4] **be born out of:** used to say that something exists as a result of a particular situation

[5] **primal:** primal feelings or behavior seem to belong to a part of people's character that is ancient and animal-like

[6] **device:** a strategy; something designed to achieve a particular purpose

Identifying Main Ideas

Match each paragraph with its main idea.

__c__ 1. paragraph 2
__d__ 2. paragraph 3
__a__ 3. paragraph 4
__e__ 4. paragraph 5
__b__ 5. paragraph 6

a. Sharing laughter helps us feel accepted by others and part of the group.
b. Laughing from being tickled evolved because it communicated friendliness.
c. Laughter is an unconscious reaction that helps people bond.
d. Laughter is more often a social signal than a reaction to humor.
e. Laughter evolved because it helped early humans cooperate and survive.

Identifying Details

Scan Reading 2 and complete each sentence with the missing information.

1. Babies begin to laugh at __three__ to __four__ months of age.
2. Researcher Robert Provine refers to laughter as a kind of "__social__ __glue__" that keeps people connected to each other.
3. In his observations, Provine found that less than __20__ percent of laughter was caused by humor.
4. People are __30__ times more likely to laugh when they are with others.
5. When early humans worked together, they were more successful at finding __food__ and fighting off __enemies__.
6. Researcher Jaak Panksepp thinks that early human laughter "evolved as a __signaling__ __device__ to highlight readiness for friendly interaction."

Making Inferences

What meaning can be inferred from the sentence? Circle the letter of the best answer.

1. We want to laugh with others because it makes us feel a bond with them, and that bond in turns gives us a sense of trust and comfort.
   a. We laugh with others when we feel uncomfortable.
   b. We don't laugh with people we don't know well.
   c. Humans have a natural desire to bond with others.
2. Mirroring other people's laughter is a way to signal to others that you feel the same way they do.
   a. Laughter is used as a form of communication.
   b. We do not always feel the same way others do.
   c. It is natural to tell others how we feel about them.
3. When we laugh, others can be certain that it is an honest reaction, and honesty is key when building and maintaining friendships.
   a. Some people laugh in a more honest way than others do.
   b. Laughing with others indirectly causes friendships to develop.
   c. It is clear to scientists why laughter is an honest reaction.
4. Sharing laughter ensured our ancestors a higher survival rate because it facilitated greater cooperation between individuals. Life back then was a numbers game, and there was power in numbers.
   a. Early humans learned to work in groups because they didn't want to live life alone.
   b. Some early humans didn't work well with others because they didn't laugh enough.
   c. The more people early humans cooperated with, the more likely they were to survive.

FROM READING TO WRITING

Vocabulary
For more practice with vocabulary, go to pages 186–187.

Reflecting on the Reading

Discuss the questions in pairs or small groups.

1. According to the reading, laughing together with others creates social bonds. What other things do you do to create or strengthen social bonds?
2. Do you agree with the author that the main reason people laugh is just because it feels good? Why or why not?

> ***Journal***
> **Choose one of your answers and write a journal entry.**

The Cause-Effect Essay

Cause-effect essays can have two different purposes. The *causal analysis essay* focuses on the causes of an event or situation. It gives reasons why something happens or has happened. Reading 1, for example, discussed reasons why people want to watch and hear about disasters. Likewise, Reading 2 focused on the causes of human laughter.

The *effect analysis essay* focuses on the effects or results of an event or situation. In an economics course, you might write about the effects of a global economy; in a psychology course, you could write about the causes or effects of stress.

Read the model essay. What three effects can urban life have on people?

MODEL

The Effects of Urban Living

1 Is living in the city natural? A look through human history might suggest so. Cities have been around for thousands of years, from the Egyptians to the Greeks to modern-day society. Cities have become such a natural place for humans to live that today more people live in cities than in the country. In America alone, nine out of ten people live in an urban area. Cities are a product of human beings. However, the experience of living in the city also has certain effects on the way people think and behave.

2 First of all, living in the city can cause people to feel anonymous. Walking around the sidewalks of a large city gives people the sense that they are one of millions. Nobody knows our name, our profession, or anything about our personal life, so we feel lost in the crowd. This can ultimately make people keep to themselves even though they are so physically close to other people, such as at the bus stop or on the subway. We might be social creatures, but the city actually seems to have the opposite effect on us sometimes.

3 At the same time as making us feel anonymous, cities can actually have an effect on our identity. People usually feel a bond with the city in which they live. People from New York are "New Yorkers" and people from Paris call themselves "Parisians." We consider ourselves "members" of the city because living in a city for a long time causes us to take on the city itself as part of our personality. People like to use their "city name" when they meet others

(continued)

because it is part of their identity. We might have control over which city we live in, but eventually, the city seems to have control over the way we feel about ourselves.

4 Finally, city living can also broaden our experiences. Large cities promote diversity. They are full of people from all around the world, who bring their own cultures and customs with them. Vietnamese restaurants sit next door to Chinese supermarkets, Colombian coffee shops, and French bakeries. Being surrounded by so many other cultures different from our own makes us more aware of the diversity in the world. After people are exposed to other cultures, they are more likely to begin to accept them, which is probably why many city dwellers enjoy being surrounded by different ways of life.

5 Cities can have a strong effect on people, including how they feel about themselves and how they feel about others. Some of this happens without our being conscious of it or our even having control over it, but that is part of what makes city living so exciting. Cities have played an important role in human history, and it is safe to say that life without them would be much less interesting.

Organizing the Cause-Effect Essay

Thesis Statement Causal analysis and effect analysis essays both show relationships between causes and effects, but their focuses are different:

- **Thesis statements for a causal analysis essay should focus on *causes*.**

EXAMPLE

CAUSES

Scientists think that laughter actually stems from our basic human need to feel close to one another, and that this evolved from an even more basic need to survive.

- **Thesis statements for an effect analysis essay should focus on *effects*.**

EXAMPLE

EFFECTS

Laughter can have a number of important psychological and physical effects on people.

Body Paragraphs The body paragraphs of a cause-effect essay should be divided according to the different causes or effects you will focus on, making one body paragraph for each one.

Essay Type	**CAUSAL ANALYSIS**	**EFFECT ANALYSIS**
Topic	why people live in cities	what effects city life has on people
Body Paragraphs	Cause 1: many jobs available Cause 2: lots of entertainment Cause 3: excellent shopping	Effect 1: makes us feel anonymous Effect 2: affects our identity Effect 3: broadens our experiences

The supporting sentences should explain each cause or effect in greater detail with examples and explanations. In cause-effect essays, it is common to include **causal chains** to show how one event leads to another event. Reading 2, a causal analysis essay, provided a causal chain to explain how laughter evolved (laughter ➛ trust ➛ cooperation ➛ finding food and fighting enemies ➛ laughter as survival ➛ laughter as a social signal). Likewise, the model essay, an effect-analysis essay, provided a causal chain that showed how being surrounded by other cultures leads to a more open mind (seeing other cultures and customs ➛ being more aware of other cultures ➛ becoming more accepting of other cultures).

Practice

A. ***Complete the chart below for the topic*** **Culture Shock.** ***List three causes or three effects for each question. Work in pairs.***

Topic: Culture Shock

CAUSE QUESTION	EFFECTS QUESTION
What causes culture shock?	**What are the effects of culture shock?**
1. *different language*	1. *feeling like a stranger*
2.	2.
3.	3.

B. ***Make a chart for each topic. List three causes or three effects for each question.***

1. **Topic:** Television
   Cause Question: Why do children watch TV?
   Effects Question: What effects does TV have on children?

2. **Topic:** English
Cause Question: Why has English become a global language?
Effects Question: What are the effects of English being a global language?

Using Cause-Effect Markers

Writers use a variety of **cause-effect markers** in their essays to make their ideas clear.

Cause Markers These verbs, phrases, and conjunctions introduce a cause.

VERBS	result from stem from be caused by } a *cause* (noun) **EXAMPLE** Satisfaction <u>results from</u> helping others.
PHRASES	as a result of because of due to } a *cause* (noun) **EXAMPLES** I feel satisfied <u>as a result of</u> helping others. <u>As a result of</u> helping others, I feel satisfied.
CONJUNCTIONS	because since } a *cause* (subject + verb) **EXAMPLES** <u>Because</u> I help others, I feel satisfied. I feel satisfied <u>because</u> I help others.

Effect Markers These verbs and transition signals introduce an effect.

VERBS	result in lead to contribute to } an *effect* (noun) **EXAMPLE** Helping others <u>results in</u> a feeling of satisfaction.
TRANSITION SIGNALS	As a result, Consequently, Therefore, Thus, } an *effect* (subject + verb) **EXAMPLE** I help others. <u>As a result</u>, I feel satisfied.

Practice

Complete the sentences with the cause-effect markers from the box. More than one answer may be possible.

~~because~~	due to	since
because of	is caused by	therefore
contribute to	result from	
consequently	result in	

1. People exercise ___*because*___ it helps them stay healthy.
2. ________________ the weather, the soccer game was canceled.
3. Driving recklessly can ________________ an accident.
4. The TV show wasn't popular. ________________, it was canceled.
5. Stress can ________________ working too many hours.
6. ________________ skydiving is so dangerous, not many people do it.
7. People are sometimes late to work ________________ heavy traffic.
8. Tigers are hunted a lot. ________________, they have become endangered.
9. Most air pollution ________________ burning coal, oil, and gas.
10. Getting a college degree can ________________ greater success in life.

WRITING ASSIGNMENT

Write a cause-effect essay. Follow the steps.

STEP 1 Get ideas.

A. Choose a topic for your essay. Check (✔) it.

❑ **Topic 1:** Why do people seek success? Write a causal analysis essay that explains the reasons behind people's desire to succeed.

❑ **Topic 2:** Studies have shown that people tell a lie two to three times a day on average. Write a causal analysis essay on the reasons why people lie.

❑ **Topic 3:** Write an effect analysis essay on the benefits of friendship.

❑ **Topic 4:** Write an effect analysis essay on different ways culture can affect people.

B. Brainstorm two or three different causes or effects to write about in your body paragraphs.

STEP 2 **Organize your ideas.**

Make an outline for your essay. Write down important supporting information such as examples and explanations that you plan to use in the body paragraphs.

STEP 3 **Write a rough draft.**

Write your essay. Use your outline from Step 2. Include vocabulary from the unit where possible.

STEP 4 **Revise your rough draft.**

Read your essay. Use the Writing Checklist to look for mistakes. Work alone or in pairs.

Writing Checklist

- ❑ Does your introduction have a clear thesis statement that states the topic and focuses on causes or effects?
- ❑ Do your body paragraphs each focus on one cause or effect?
- ❑ Does your conclusion restate the thesis in different words?
- ❑ Did you use vocabulary from the unit appropriately in your writing?
- ❑ Did use you include cause-effect markers appropriately in your essay?

STEP 5 **Edit your writing.**

A. Edit your essay. Use the correction symbols on page 173. Correct any mistakes in capitalization, punctuation, spelling, verb tense, or the use of participial adjectives.

Participial adjectives are formed from verbs. Present participial adjectives (*-ing*) indicate a cause.

EXAMPLE

PRESENT PARTICIPIAL ADJECTIVE

exciting

City life can be ~~excited~~.

Past participial adjectives (*-ed*) indicate an effect or result.

EXAMPLE

PAST PARTICIPIAL ADJECTIVE

excited

The children were ~~exciting~~ about going to the zoo.

B. Work in pairs. Exchange essays and check each other's work.

STEP 6 **Write a final copy.**

Correct your mistakes. Copy your final essay and give it to your instructor.

UNIT

8

Privacy

In this unit you will:

- read articles about tracking technology
- learn to identify supporting and opposing points in a reading
- organize and write an argumentative essay

PRE-READING 1

Discussion

Discuss the questions in pairs or small groups.

1. Look at the picture. What is this man's job?
2. Do you think businesses should videotape their employees? Why or why not?
3. What types of technology are used to keep people safe? What kinds of technology can be dangerous to people?

Vocabulary

Read the article. Match each boldfaced word or phrase with the definition in the box. Write the letter.

GPS

GPS, which stands for Global Positioning System, is a term that is used a lot today. GPS **is based on** (1 b) technology that was developed by the United States space program. The system uses satellites in space to locate objects on Earth. With a GPS receiver, a person's location and movements on earth can be **monitored** (2 i). Today, some cars are installed with a GPS computer map that **is devoted to** (3 d) helping people get around when driving. Using the technology, drivers are able to **verify** (4 C) their exact location in case they get lost.

GPS signals are accurate and reliable with only a few **exceptions** (5 g), such as when signals from other electronics like TVs and radios interfere with the GPS signal. Another **drawback** (6 a) is that GPS signals can be altered if they hit tall objects like buildings and mountains. Today, scientists are **pursuing** (7 f) ways to improve GPS technology to ensure that the signals are always accurate.

Because GPS technology is able to track people's movements as well, some have argued that it could **compromise** (8 e) people's privacy if it is used by the wrong people. They worry that people might follow the movements of others without their **consent** (9 h). Because of this, countries are looking at ways to improve the safety of GPS technology.

a. disadvantage of a situation, product, etc.
b. be developed from particular information or facts as a starting point
c. find out if a fact, statement, etc., is correct or true
d. be used for a specific purpose
e. harm or damage something in some way, for example by behaving in a way that does not match a legal or moral standard
f. continue doing an activity or trying to achieve something over a long period of time
g. someone or something that is not included in a rule, or does not follow the expected pattern, etc.
h. permission to do something
i. carefully watch, listen to, or examine something or someone over a period of time

READING 1

Future with Nowhere to Hide

1 We're all too familiar with the concept of technology as a double-edged sword,[1] and wireless technology is no **exception**. Yes, the idea of getting rid of wires and cables is exciting: We can go anywhere and still maintain intimate contact with our work, our loved ones, and our real-time sports scores. But the same persistent connectedness may well lead us toward a future where our cell phones tag and track us like FedEx packages, sometimes with our permission and sometimes when we're not aware.

2 To see how this might work, check out Worktrack, a product of Aligo, a Mountain View, California producer of "mobile services." The system is sold to employers who want to computerize and **verify** time logs[2] of their workers in the field. The first customers are in the heating and air-conditioning business. Workers have cell phones equipped with GPS that show their exact locations to computers in the back office. Their movements can be checked against the "Geo Fence" that employers draw up, marking the area where their work is situated. (This sounds uncomfortably like the pet-control technology, those "invisible fences" that give dogs a shock if they go beyond the backyard.)

3 "It they're not in the right area, they're really not working," says Aligo CEO, Robert Smith. "A notification will come to the back office that they're not where they should be." The system also tracks how fast the workers drive, so the employer can verify to insurance companies that no one is speeding. All of this is perfectly legal, of course, as employers have the right to **monitor** their workers. Smith says that workers like the technology because it ensures they get credit for the time they spend on the job.

4 Worktrack is only one of a number of services **devoted to** tracking humans. Parents use similar ways to make sure their kids are safe. In addition, many drivers are already allowing safety monitors to use GPS on their travels. Look for the practice to really explode as mobile-phone makers comply with[3] a law stating that all handsets must include GPS that pinpoints the owner's location.

5 The prospect of being tracked "turns the freedom of mobile telephony upside down,"[4] says Marc Rotenberg of the Electronic Privacy Information Center. His concern is government surveillance[5] and the storage of one's movements in databases. In fact, if information from the GPS signals is kept, it would be easy to keep a record of an individual's movements over a period of years (just as phone records are kept). An even darker view is proposed by two academics

(continued)

[1] **double-edged sword:** an expression used to say that something has both advantages and disadvantages

[2] **time log:** an official record showing the hours an employee has worked

[3] **comply with:** do what you must do or are asked to do

[4] **turn (something) upside down:** do something that makes a way of understanding something change completely

[5] **surveillance:** the act of carefully watching a person or place because they may be connected with criminal activities

who wrote a paper warning the beginning of "geoslavery." Its definition is "a practice in which one entity, the master . . . monitors and exerts control over the physical location of another individual to routinely control time, location, speed, and direction for each and every movement of the slave."

6 My guess is that the widespread adoption of tracking won't be done against our will[6] but initially with our **consent**. As with other double-edged tools, the benefits will be immediately apparent, while the **drawbacks** for privacy emerge gradually. The first attraction will **be based on** fear: In addition to employers' keeping workers in tow,[7] Mom and Dad will insist their teenagers have GPS devices so parents can follow them throughout their day. The second stage will come as location-based services, from navigation to "friend-finding" (some systems tell you when online buddies are in shouting range), make our lives more efficient and pleasurable.

7 Sooner or later, though, we will realize that information taken from our movements has **compromised** our "locational privacy"—a term that may become familiar only when there is no more. "I don't see much that will bring about [protections] in the short term," says Mark Monmonier, author of *Spying with Maps*. He thinks that we'll only get serious about this after we suffer some major privacy violations.[8] But if nothing is done, **pursuing** our love affair with wireless will result in the loss of a freedom—the license to get lost. Here's a new battle cry for the wireless era: Don't Geo-Fence me in.

[6] **will:** what someone wants to happen in a particular situation

[7] **in tow:** following closely behind someone or something

[8] **violation:** an action that breaks a law, agreement, principle, rule, etc.

Identifying Main Ideas

Read each question. Circle the letter of the best answer.

1. What is the author's main opinion of wireless technology?
   a. He thinks companies should use GPS to track the movements of their employees.
   b. He hopes that wireless technology will help parents keep track of their children.
   c. He believes wireless technology could compromise people's privacy and personal freedom.
   d. He is completely certain that using GPS technology will lead to the beginning of geoslavery.
2. What is the main idea of paragraph 2?
   a. Some employers use GPS technology to track workers via their cell phones.
   b. Heating and air-conditioning businesses were the first companies to use Worktrack.

c. GPS technology can help someone identify the exact location of another person.

d. Some workers disagree with employers who use GPS technology to track them.

3. What is the main idea of paragraph 3?

a. Both employers and employees see benefits in tracking workers.

b. GPS systems can be used to monitor how fast people drive.

c. Workers with a GPS-equipped cell phone should not speed.

d. Insurance companies like businesses that use tracking technology.

4. What is the main idea of paragraph 5?

a. Governments can use databases to keep private information about their citizens.

b. Geoslavery occurs when one person monitors the movements of another person.

c. It is still unknown how much wireless tracking will compromise our freedom.

d. Information taken from a GPS signal can be saved for many years.

5. What is the main idea of paragraph 6?

a. Wireless tracking may or may not become popular in the future.

b. Most parents require their children to have GPS devices.

c. Parents can follow their children easily using a GPS device.

d. Wireless tracking devices will seem to have benefits at first.

Identifying Details

Mark the statements* T *(true) or* F *(false).

____ 1. It is illegal for companies to track their workers using GPS.

____ 2. "Geo Fences" are drawn up by cell-phone companies.

____ 3. All new handsets in the United States are equipped with GPS.

____ 4. Fear will cause parents to begin to use tracking technology.

____ 5. GPS technology is only used by governments and businesses.

Making Inferences

The answers to the following questions are not stated directly in the reading. What information can be inferred to answer the questions? Work in pairs.

1. Why would parents want to track their children?
2. Why are people not familiar with the term "locational privacy" yet?
3. What kinds of privacy violations could result from wireless tracking?

READING SKILL

Identifying Arguments and Counterarguments

When writers discuss a controversial subject, they usually consider *both* sides of the issue, including reasons why they support an issue and the reasons why others might oppose it. Effective writers give the opposing opinion—called the **counterargument**—to show why it is less valid than their own. This makes the author's **argument**, or personal opinion, stronger and more believable.

When reading an opinion-based text, it is important to be able to distinguish between arguments and counterarguments.

EXAMPLE

> Parents have a responsibility to monitor what their children are doing on the Internet. Many children, especially teenagers, believe that they have a right to privacy even though they are not yet adults. Furthermore, they argue that parents monitoring their Internet usage can lead to a lack of trust. However, until children are old enough to live on their own, parents should have the right to see how their children spend their time on the Web. Most monitor them because they want to make sure they are safe, not because they are interested in their private affairs. As the old saying goes, "It's better to be safe than sorry."

The underlined sentences in the paragraph support the counterargument—that children believe they have a right to Internet privacy. They give points which people could use to disagree with the writer. The double-underlined sentences are reasons that support the author's argument—that parents should monitor their children's use of the Internet.

Practice

Look at these points from Reading 1. Which argument do they support? Mark the sentences A (author's argument) or C (counterargument).

____ 1. GPS tracking will compromise people's "locational privacy."

____ 2. Employee tracking ensures workers get credit for the time they work.

C 3. Businesses have the right to monitor their workers.

A 4. Wireless tracking could lead to the beginning of a new form of slavery.

C 5. Employers can use GPS tracking to verify their workers aren't speeding.

A 6. Overusing wireless technology could result in an individual's loss of freedom.

VOCABULARY SKILL

Using Noun Suffixes

Suffixes can be added to the end of certain verbs to change them into nouns.

EXAMPLE

VERB

Some people don't want to <u>adopt</u> wireless tracking technology in the workplace.

NOUN

Experts predict that the <u>adoption</u> of GPS tracking devices will become more common in the workplace.

Look at the verbs and their suffixes *-ion* and *-cation*.

EXAMPLES	SPELLINGS
adopt—adopt<u>ion</u> protect—protect<u>ion</u>	Many verbs that end in *-t* add *-ion*.
educate—educat<u>ion</u> navigate—navigat<u>ion</u>	Verbs that end in *-ate* drop the *e* and add *-ion*.
verify—verifi<u>cation</u> identify—identifi<u>cation</u>	Verbs that end in *-ify* change the *y* to *i* and add *-cation*.

Practice

A. Use the suffixes from the chart to change the verbs into nouns.

1. attract attraction
2. communicate Communication
3. direct direction
4. specify specification
5. create creation
6. classify classification
7. modify modification
8. perfect perfection

B. Complete each sentence. Circle the correct word form.

1. Many stores in Europe are (adopting / adoption) security cameras to prevent people from stealing.
2. Police departments can use fingerprints to (verify / verification) a person's identity.
3. No one can guarantee the total (protect / protection) of people's information on the Internet.
4. When traveling to another country, it is important to carry proper (identify / identification), such as a passport.
5. GPS (navigate / navigation) systems are no longer used only by governments. Today everyday people can buy GPS devices.
6. (Educating / Education) people about the pros and cons of tracking technology is important because it can affect them directly.

FROM READING TO WRITING

> ***Journal***
> Choose one of your answers and write a journal entry.

Reflecting on the Reading

Discuss the questions in pairs or small groups.

1. Do you think that companies should track their workers? Why or why not?
2. Do you think wireless tracking will become more common in the future? Explain.
3. Write your own definition of the word *privacy*. How is it similar to or different from the dictionary definition?

Discussion

Discuss the questions in pairs or small groups.

1. At what age should parents allow their children to go out on their own? Why?
2. Are you for or against parents using tracking devices on children? Explain.

Vocabulary

Read the boldfaced words and their definitions. Then complete the article with the correct words or phrases. Change the form of words as needed.

be linked to: be connected to something or someone else
convinced: certain that something is true
dilemma: a situation in which you have to make a difficult choice between two or more actions
expand: become larger in size, number, or amount
invasive: involving an intrusion of somebody's privacy or rights
in this case: in a particular situation or problem
technique: a method or way of doing something
transmit: send or pass something from one person, place, or thing to another
trustworthy: able to be trusted and depended on

Computer Cookies

Most people associate the word *cookie* with a sweet treat. However, because of the Internet, the definition of the word has (1) ____________ to mean more than just something to eat. "Cookies" are found on people's computers, too—they are pieces of information that (2) ____________ websites you have visited. When you visit a website, the site leaves a cookie on your computer that will help your computer recognize the website the next time you visit it.

Many people believe cookies are beneficial because they make Web surfing faster, but others are not (3) ____________. These people argue that cookies are too (4) ____________ because they can track which websites you visit, how often you visit them, and what you do on them. In reality, most of the information that your cookies (5) ____________ back to websites is used correctly; however, not all websites are safe. Some websites, such as school and government websites, are more (6) ____________ than others. Others can't and shouldn't be trusted.

Luckily, deciding which websites to visit and which to avoid does not have to be a major (7) ____________. You can use your computer's security settings to control cookies. This is the most common and useful (8) ____________ for controlling them. The computer will allow cookies for trusted sites but alert you about sites it feels are not safe. (9) ____________, it is usually best to trust the program and not visit the site. You don't want to allow any cookie that might bite you back!

READING 2

More Parents Going High-Tech to Track Kids

1 CHICAGO (AP)—**In this case**, it isn't Big Brother[1] who's watching—it's Big Mother (or Father). Increasingly, parents are using high-tech methods to track everything from where their children are and how far they are driving to what they buy, what they eat, and whether they've shown up for class.

2 Often, the gadget involved is a simple cell phone that **transmits** location data. The details get delivered by e-mail, cell-phone text message, or the Web. Other times, the tech tool is a debit-like card used at a school lunch counter, or a device that lets parents know not only how far and fast the car is going, but also whether their child has been braking too hard or making jackrabbit starts.[2]

3 Ted Schmidt, a father in suburban Burr Ridge, Illinois, uses the cell phone method to track his four children, including two in college. "Here's the story," Schmidt told them when he decided to begin tracking them about a year ago. "24/7, I can tell where your phone is, what speed it's going. . . . So (even) days later, I can look and see that 'Oh my gosh, you were going 80 miles an hour on the Interstate at two o'clock in the morning.'" It might sound **invasive**, but Schmidt is **convinced** it's keeping his kids safer—partly because they know they're being watched.

[1] **Big Brother:** any person, organization, or system that seems to want to control people's lives and restrict their freedom

[2] **jackrabbit start:** beginning to drive in a sudden, rapid way

His 15-year-old son, Noah, who's been caught a few places he wasn't supposed to be, isn't nearly as pleased. "It's annoying," the high school sophomore complains, and "it gives the parents too much control."

4 The Schmidts' older daughters are, however, more accepting. Ciarra Schmidt, a New York University freshman, likes to know her parents could find her in an emergency. "You never know what could happen," the 18-year-old says. "It's a nice kind of security blanket." The Schmidts use a service called Teen Arrive Alive, one of a few companies that work with Nextel wireless phones and a tracking service from uLocate Communications, Inc. Other devices that track on-the-go kids include the Wherifone, a specialized locator phone that uses the Global Positioning System, and the CarChip, a device about the size of two nine-volt batteries stacked together that, installed in a vehicle, monitors speed, distance, and driving habits.

5 Interest in the United States is growing quickly, as it already has in other countries—Canada and the United Kingdom included. Teen Arrive Alive, which began offering its tracking service in May 2004, now has subscribers in every state and is particularly popular in the South and the East, company officials say. These days, it's just one way technology is helping parents monitor their kids.

6 Georgia-based Mealpay.com began two years ago, for instance, as a way for parents to electronically prepay school lunches. Now, at the request of some parents, the service allows them to monitor what kids order in the cafeteria. Meanwhile, Boston-based MobileLime allows teens to use cell phones to buy items at fast-food restaurants, grocery stores, and other participating retailers. The cell phone **is linked to** a credit or prepaid card, so parents can check.

Then there's "alerts" from U.K.–based Langtree SkillsCenter Ltd. Parents are notified by text message, e-mail, or phone about whether a student has shown up for class, and they can get progress reports (good and bad) on schoolwork. Just starting up, the company has signed about 10 U.K. schools so far and is **expanding** to the United States.

7 Parenting experts have mixed views on such **techniques**. In general, monitoring a child—knowing where they're going, who they're hanging out with—is a good thing, says Christy Buchanan, an associate professor of psychology at Wake Forest University in North Carolina. She also notes that some teens are more **trustworthy** and less likely to take risks than others. "But parents have to strike some balance between knowing what their kids are up to without the adolescent feeling like they're having their every move controlled," says Buchanan, who is involved in a multiyear study of teens and parents. "Parents shouldn't fool themselves[3] into thinking that they can keep their kids from making mistakes, which is part of growing up and learning."

8 Sometimes, young people find ways around technological monitoring. Buchanan knows students who simply leave their GPS-enabled cell phones under their dorm room beds or turn them off for extended periods of time. Kate Kelly, author of *The Complete Idiot's Guide to Parenting a Teenager*, doesn't blame them. "Normal spouses don't hire private detectives to track the

(continued)

[3]**fool yourself:** try to make yourself believe something that you know is not really true

whereabouts[4] of their mates, and parents who have done their jobs in establishing good relationships with their teens shouldn't be using extraordinary high-tech devices to follow their teens," Kelly says. "You've got to create a relationship built on trust, not fear."

9 Some manufacturers of tracking products see the point—to a point. "It certainly is a fine line between care and overprotection—and parents face this **dilemma** all the time," says Gavin Biggs, an "alerts" spokesman. "But is there any other time where your child is out of your control for seven, eight hours a day, five days a week, 40 weeks a year?"

10 Others make no apologies. "Spying on kids is not the motive," says Teen Arrive Alive spokesman, Jack Church, who lost a teenage son in a car crash. "To me, as a parent, this is peace of mind. It's saying, 'I want you to stay alive to see your graduation.'" That's one reason Schmidt plans to continue using the service. "As much as (my son) protests and hates it, we're the only parents who know what's going on," he says. "I think kids want to know their parents care."

[4] **whereabouts:** the place or area where someone or something is

Identifying Main Ideas

Scan Reading 2. Make a chart like the one below and complete it for each paragraph listed.

ARGUMENTS THAT SUPPORT PARENTS TRACKING CHILDREN	ARGUMENTS THAT OPPOSE PARENTS TRACKING CHILDREN
Para 3: *parents can monitor driving habits*	Para 3: *parents have too much control*
Para 4:	Para 7:
Para 6:	Para 8:
Para 10:	

Identifying Details

Match each company with the tracking service it offers.

___ 1. Teen Arrive Alive

___ 2. CarChip

c 3. Mealpay.com

a 4. MobileLime

e 5. Langtree SkillsCenter Ltd

a. monitors kids' credit card purchases at restaurants and stores b. locates and tracks kids through their cell phones c. monitors what children order at school cafeterias d. monitors vehicle speed, distance, and driving habits e. alerts parents about their child's school attendance and progress reports

Making Inferences

Infer what the writer would say is true even though it is not directly stated. Check (✔) each statement the writer would agree with.

✓ 1. Using tracking devices can result in a lack of trust between parents and children.

___ 2. Children who live in Canada are safer than those who live in the United States.

✓ 3. Some parents believe that they can control their children all of the time.

✓ 4. Parents should monitor children who are more likely to take risks.

___ 5. Paying for a tracking service is too expensive for most parents.

___ 6. The author strongly supports parents tracking their children.

FROM READING TO WRITING

Journal
Choose one of your answers and write a journal entry.

Reflecting on the Reading

Discuss the questions in pairs or small groups.

1. Now that you have looked at Reading 2, has your opinion about tracking children changed? Explain.
2. Should schools be allowed to track children outside of the classroom or employers be allowed to track employees outside of work? Why or why not?

WRITING

Vocabulary
For more practice with vocabulary, go to pages 188–189.

The Argumentative Essay

The **argumentative essay** focuses on a controversial topic or on a subject about which people disagree. Writers of an argumentative essay must give their position on a topic (supporting or opposing) and present reasons that support their belief. In Reading 1, for example, the writer explained why he or she felt GPS tracking technology was an invasion of privacy. In a sociology class, students might write an essay on whether they believe the media is a positive or negative force in society. Students studying law might write an argumentative essay on how they think governments should handle illegal immigration.

Read the model essay.

MODEL

Tag, You're It!

1 Most people have no idea what RFID stands for, despite its ever-growing use. Radio Frequency Identification or RFID, is a technology that uses a tiny computer chip connected to an antenna. Together they make an RFID tag. The tag can be tracked by an electronic reader that can monitor its location. This information can then be stored in a computer database for any period of time. Major retailers like Wal-Mart have been using RFID chips to track shipments of products to their stores. Recently, retailers, credit card companies, and even governments have realized the powerful benefits of RFID in tracking not just objects, but also people. However, using RFID to track people and their purchases would compromise our privacy and security. Because of this, I feel the technology should be banned altogether.

2 First of all, using RFID in stores puts people's privacy at risk. When you buy a product with an RFID tag, the store can continue to monitor the chip's location after your purchase. In other words, no matter where you go—home, work, or out to dinner—your location can be identified. The benefit to stores is that they can see if specific products can be linked to specific neighborhoods. They could then change their marketing to target these areas. However, this is not information that stores should be able to keep about their customers. The clothes we wear, the books we read, and the videos we watch should remain private information. We wouldn't give this information to a stranger, so why should we give it to companies—especially without our consent?

3 Using RFID could mean a loss to people's safety and security as well. More and more credit cards have a wireless RFID tag, so consumers don't have to swipe their cards anymore. Instead, the card number is transmitted from a tiny antenna through the air to a reader. This means that anyone with a reader nearby could take this information. With the right technology, someone could steal this information, take your identity, and buy products in your name. Credit cards that use RFID are simply not worth the risk.

4 Supporters of RFID say it is giving people what they want—convenience. Not having to swipe a credit card saves time. In today's fast-paced world, saving time is a good thing. However, we have to ask ourselves what is more important—convenience or personal security and privacy? The truth is that RFID is an invasive technology that prevents us from keeping our personal information private and safe. In this case, security needs to be given more importance than convenience.

5 Today, billions of RFID tags are being sold, and businesses are spending billions of dollars to use RFID tags to track both products and people. All of this is happening without the public even knowing about it. If RFID is not outlawed soon, it may not be long before the term "private information" no longer means anything. Privacy is a right, and it is one most of us would like to keep.

Practice

Answer the questions about the model essay.

1. Look at the introduction. What is RFID and how does it work?
2. Look at the first and second body paragraphs. How do they support the author's thesis statement?
3. Look at the conclusion. What are the author's final thoughts on the topic?

WRITING SKILL

Organizing the Argumentative Essay

Introduction Begin the introduction with an interesting lead. Define any necessary words, and identify why the topic is controversial. The thesis statement for an argumentative essay should state the topic and identify the author's opinion about it.

EXAMPLE

Using RFID to track people and their purchases would compromise our privacy and security. Because of this, I feel the technology should be banned altogether.

Body Paragraphs The first few body paragraphs should identify the reasons why you support or oppose the issue. Write one paragraph for each reason. Make sure to include specific details to support your ideas, such as facts, examples, and detailed explanations.

The final body paragraph should include three things: the counterargument, the explanation of the counterargument, and your refutation.

- The **counterargument** is the opposing opinion about your topic. This "opposite" view is often introduced with the phrases *Some people argue . . .* or *Supporters/Opponents of . . .*

EXAMPLE

Supporters of RFID technology say it is giving people what they want—convenience.

- The **explanation of the counterargument** identifies reasons why some people support the opposing argument.

EXAMPLE

Not having to swipe a credit card saves time. In today's fast-paced world, saving time is a good thing.

- The **refutation** is your response to the counterargument. Here, you must show the weaknesses in the counterargument. You need to explain why the reader should believe your position and not the opposing position. Refutations often begin with transition signals like *however* or *on the other hand*.

EXAMPLE

However, we have to ask ourselves what is more important—convenience or personal security and privacy? The truth is that RFID is an invasive technology that prevents us from keeping our personal information private and safe. In this case, security needs to be given more importance than convenience.

Conclusion In your conclusion, restate your opinion about the issue and summarize your main points. Finish with strong final thoughts that will help persuade readers to agree with your position.

Practice

A. *Complete the chart below for the topic* **Animals should be used in research.** *List three Supporting Reasons and three Opposing Reasons. Then compare answers with a partner.*

Topic: Animals should be used in research.

SUPPORTING REASONS	OPPOSING REASONS
1. *It's wrong to test on humans.*	1. *Medical tests can hurt animals.*
2.	2.
3.	3.

B. *Make a chart for each topic. List three Supporting Reasons and three Opposing Reasons.*

1. **Topic:** Children under 13 should carry cell phones.
2. **Topic:** Attendance should be mandatory in college classes.

C. *Finish each paragraph by writing a refutation to the counterargument.*

1. Many people argue that they should have the right to talk on their cell phones when driving. They feel that what they do in their own car is their own business. However, ____
____
____
____.

2. Opponents of building new public transportation systems in American cities believe they will be a waste of money. They think that people will continue to use their cars to get around because driving is more convenient than taking a bus, for example. This may be true for some people, but ____
____
____
____.

WRITING ASSIGNMENT

Write an argumentative essay. Follow the steps.

STEP 1 Get ideas.

A. Choose a topic for your essay. Check (✔) it.

- ❑ **Topic 1:** Are you for or against parents using tracking technology on children?
- ❑ **Topic 2:** Do you believe the Internet is a threat to privacy?
- ❑ **Topic 3:** Do you support or oppose the installation of "mom cams" (surveillance cameras used in public areas on campus for parents to watch) on college campuses?
- ❑ **Topic 4:** Some countries are starting to keep DNA (genetic) records of their citizens. Do you support or oppose countries keeping a national DNA database?

B. List reasons why people support and oppose your position.

STEP 2 Organize your ideas.

Make an outline for your essay. Choose ideas from Step 1.

STEP 3 Write a rough draft.

Write your essay. Write one body paragraph for each reason that supports your opinion. The final body paragraph should include the counterargument, explanation of the counterargument, and the refutation. Use your outline from Step 2. Include vocabulary from the unit where possible.

STEP 4 Revise your rough draft.

Read your essay. Use the Writing Checklist to look for mistakes. Work alone or in pairs.

Writing Checklist

- ❑ Does your introduction give background information about the topic and identify why the topic is controversial?
- ❑ Does your thesis statement indicate your position on the topic?
- ❑ Do your body paragraphs support your thesis statement?
- ❑ Do your body paragraphs include the counterargument, explanation of the counterargument, and a refutation?
- ❑ Does your conclusion restate your opinion and summarize your main points?

STEP 5 Edit your writing.

A. Edit your essay. Use the correction symbols on page 173. Correct any mistakes in capitalization, punctuation, spelling, verb-tense, or the use of adjective clauses.

EXAMPLE

ADJECTIVE CLAUSE

RFID tags that stores use ~~them~~ can be expensive.

B. Work in pairs. Exchange essays and check each other's work.

STEP 6 Write a final copy.

Correct your mistakes. Copy your final essay and give it to your instructor.

UNIT

9

Literature

In this unit you will:

- read a short story by Oscar Wilde
- learn to recognize themes in literature
- organize and write a thematic analysis essay

PRE-READING 1

Discussion

Discuss the questions in pairs or small groups.

1. What would you do with a million dollars?
2. Do you think the rich should help the poor? Why or why not?
3. What is more important—love or money? Explain.

Vocabulary

Read the article. Match each boldfaced word or phrase with the definition in the box. Write the letter.

Oscar Wilde

Author Oscar Wilde lived from 1854 to 1900. He was born in Dublin, Ireland to wealthy parents. Wilde was lucky to have wealthy parents during this time. For the rich, life was good, but for the poor, it was **cruel** (1____). They received little help from the government and lived in unhealthy conditions. Even though so many people were **miserable** (2____), the rich did not want to help the poor. Most cared only about their own private **affairs** (3____). Oscar Wilde's father, however, was different. He **pitied** (4____) the poor so much that he built Dublin's first hospital for the poor, which still exists today.

Because his family had money, Oscar Wilde went to the best schools. Wilde was a very **clever** (5____) student, and he had a successful college career. His professors at Ireland's Trinity College **were** so **fond of** (6____) his work that they awarded him the highest academic honor for literature students. After Trinity, Wilde studied at Oxford University in England. Here he moved away from his **former** (7____) focus on classic literature and began writing pieces that were influenced by modern themes.

Wilde's greatest work was a **charming** (8____) play entitled *The Importance of Being Earnest*. It put theater audiences in great **spirits** (9____) because of its intelligent humor, which often made fun of the rich. The play has been an **astonishing** (10____) success. Audiences still go to see theater productions of the play today, more than a hundred years after it was written.

a. so surprising that it is difficult to believe
b. very pleasing or attractive
c. able to learn and understand things quickly; smart
d. like someone or something
e. happening or existing before
f. extremely unhappy, for example, because you feel sick or badly treated
g. feel sorry for people because they are in a very bad situation
h. very hard or brutal, causing suffering
i. things related to your personal life, your financial situation, etc.
j. the way people feel at any time, for example, if they are cheerful or sad

READING 1

The Model Millionaire

By Oscar Wilde

Part 1

1 Unless one is wealthy, there is no use in being a **charming** person. The poor should be ordinary and practical. It is better to have a permanent income than to be interesting. These are the great truths of modern life which Hughie Erskine never realized. Poor Hughie! He was not, we must admit, a man of great intelligence. He never said a **clever** or even an unkind thing in his life. But then he was wonderfully good-looking, with his brown hair, his clear-cut features, and his gray eyes. He was as popular with men as he was with women, and he had every quality except that of making money. His father, on his death, had left him his sword[1] and a *History of the Peninsular War* in 15 parts. Hughie hung the first above his mirror, put the second on a shelf, and lived on two hundred pounds[2] a year that an old aunt allowed him. He had tried everything. He had bought and sold shares for six months, but how could he succeed among experienced men? He had been a tea trader for a little longer, but he had soon tired of that. Then he had tried selling wine, but nobody bought any. At last he became nothing, a charming, useless young man with perfect features and no profession.

2 To make matters worse, he was in love. The girl he loved was Laura Merton, the daughter of a **former** army officer who had lost his temper[3] and his health in India, and had never found either of them again. Hughie loved her so much that he was ready to kiss her feet; and Laura loved him too. They were the best-looking pair in London, and had no money at all. Her father **was** very **fond of** Hughie, but would not hear of any marriage plans.

3 "Come to me, my boy, when you have got ten thousand pounds of your own, and we will see about it," he used to say.

4 One morning, Hughie called in to see a great friend of his, Alan Trevor. Trevor was a painter. Of course, few people are not these days. But he was also an artist, and artists are rather rare. He was a strange, rough man, with a spotty face and an overgrown red beard. But when he took up the brush, he was a real master, and his pictures were very popular. He had been much attracted by Hughie at first, it must be admitted, just because of his personal charm. "The only people a painter should know," he used to say, "are people who are both beautiful and stupid, people who are a pleasure to look at and restful to talk to." But after he got to know Hughie better, he liked him quite as much for his bright, cheerful spirits, and his generous,[4] carefree nature, and had asked him to visit whenever he liked.

5 When Hughie came in, he found Trevor putting the finishing touches to a wonderful

[1] **sword:** a weapon with a long, pointed blade and a handle, used in past times

[2] **pound:** the standard unit of money in the United Kingdom

[3] **lose your temper:** suddenly become so angry that you cannot control yourself

[4] **generous:** sympathetic in the way you deal with people, and tending not to criticize them, get angry, or treat them in a way that is not nice

life-size picture of a beggar.[5] The beggar himself was standing on a raised platform[6] in a corner of the room. He was a tired old man with a lined face and a sad expression. Over his shoulder was thrown a rough brown coat, all torn and full of holes; his thick boots were old and mended,[7] and with one hand he leaned on a rough stick, while with the other he held out his old hat for money.

6 "What an **astonishing** model!" whispered Hughie, as he shook hands with his friend.

7 "An astonishing model?" shouted Trevor at the top of his voice; "I should think so! Such beggars are not met with every day. Good heavens! What a picture Rembrandt would have made of him!"

8 "Poor old man!" said Hughie. "How **miserable** he looks! But I suppose, to you painters, his face is a fortune."

9 "Certainly," replied Trevor, "you don't want a beggar to look happy, do you?"

10 "How much does a model get for being painted?" asked Hughie, as he found himself a comfortable seat.

11 "A shilling[8] an hour."

12 "And how much do you get for your picture, Alan?"

13 "Oh, for this I get two thousand pounds."

14 "Well, I think the model should have a share," cried Hughie, laughing; "he works quite as hard as you do."

15 "Nonsense,[9] nonsense! Look at the trouble of laying on the paint, and standing all day in front of the picture! It's easy, Hughie, for you to talk. But you mustn't talk; I'm busy. Smoke a cigarette, and keep quiet."

16 After some time the servant came in, and told Trevor that the frame maker wanted to speak to him.

17 "Don't run away, Hughie," he said, as he went out, "I will be back in a moment."

18 The old beggar took advantage of Trevor's absence to rest for a moment. He looked so miserable that Hughie **pitied** him, and felt in his pockets to see what money he had. All he could find was a pound and some pennies. "Poor old man," he thought, "he needs it more than I do, but I shan't[10] have much money myself for a week or two"; and he walked across the room and slipped the pound into the beggar's hand.

19 The old man jumped, and a faint[11] smile passed across his old lips. "Thank you, sir," he said, "thank you."

20 Then Trevor arrived, and Hughie left, a little red in the face at what he had done. He spent the day with Laura, who was charmingly cross[12] that he had given away a pound, and had to walk home because he had no money for transport.

21 That night he went to his club at about 11 o'clock, and found Trevor sitting by himself in the smoking room.

22 "Well, Alan, did you finish the picture all right?" he asked.

(continued)

[5] **beggar:** someone who lives by asking people for food and money

[6] **platform:** a raised floor or stage for people to stand on

[7] **mend:** repair a hole or tear, especially in a piece of clothing

[8] **shilling:** a unit of money used in past times in the United Kingdom. There were 20 shillings in a pound.

[9] **nonsense:** ideas, opinions, statements, etc. that are not true or that seem very stupid

[10] **shan't:** Old English contraction for shall not

[11] **faint:** difficult to see, hear, smell, etc.

[12] **cross:** angry or annoyed, used more frequently in British English

23 "Finished and framed, my boy," answered Trevor; "and, by the way, that old model you saw has become very fond of you. I had to tell him all about you—who you are, where you live, what your income is, what hopes you have. . . ."

24 "My dear Alan," cried Hughie, "I shall probably find him waiting for me when I go home. But, of course, you are only joking. Poor old man! I wish I could do something for him. I think it is terrible that anyone should be so miserable. I have got piles of old clothes at home—do you think he would like any of them? His clothes were falling to bits."

25 "But he looks wonderful in them," said Trevor. "I would never want to paint him in good clothes. But I'll tell him of your offer."

Identifying Main Ideas

These events from the story are not in the correct sequence. Number them in order 1–6.

__6__ 1. Hughie went to his club and saw Trevor again.
__4__ 2. Hughie gave the beggar a pound.
__2__ 3. Trevor was painting a picture of a beggar.
__3__ 4. Trevor stopped painting to speak to the frame maker.
__1__ 5. Hughie went to visit Alan Trevor.
__5__ 6. Hughie went to see Laura.

Identifying Details

Scan Reading 1. Then complete each sentence with the correct amount.

1. Hughie lived on __two hundred pounds__ a year from his aunt.
2. Hughie couldn't marry Laura until he had saved __ten thousand Pounds__.
3. Trevor will earn __two thousand pounds__ for his picture of the beggar.
4. Trevor pays his models __a shilling__ for one hour of work.
5. Hughie gave the beggar __a pound__.

Making Inferences

The answers to the questions are not directly stated in the reading. What information can be inferred to answer the questions? Work in pairs.

1. What do you think the difference is between a painter and an artist?
2. Why doesn't Alan Trevor pay his models more than a shilling an hour?
3. Why does Hughie think the beggar will be waiting for him at his house?

Recognizing Themes in Literature

All literature, whether it is a poem, short story, or novel, reflects an author's own views on society and the human experience. **Themes** are usually generalizations about life or universal topics, such as love, money, beauty, honesty, and happiness. They also may represent an author's own values or conclusions that are based on his or her own personal experience or observations.

Recognizing themes requires you to look for "deeper meanings" in the text. Authors do not explicitly state their themes in their stories; instead, readers must infer the themes by analyzing the plot and the characters of a story and identifying what the characters and plot suggest about the author's viewpoints on life. Sometimes an author will promote, or support, a particular kind of behavior, attitude, or idea about life; other times, an author might suggest a behavior, attitude, or idea that he or she disagrees with.

Practice

Discuss these questions about themes in pairs or small groups. Take notes on your discussion, and share your answers with the rest of the class.

1. **Theme:** *generosity*
   Alan Trevor earns two thousand pounds for a painting but only pays the beggar a shilling an hour. What does Hughie think about his lack of generosity? What does this suggest about Wilde's opinion on being generous?
2. **Theme:** *compassion*
   How does Hughie show compassion toward the beggar? How do you think Wilde feels about being compassionate toward others?
3. **Theme:** *the power of money*
   How does being poor affect Hughie's love life? What does this suggest about the influence that money has on people's choices in life?

Identifying Formal and Informal Synonyms

In English, a single word may have many synonyms. Some synonyms will be used in formal speech and writing, such as a speech or an academic essay. Others will be used more often in conversations or informal writing such as an e-mail to a friend. The word *rich*, for example, is used in more informal situations. *Wealthy* is a more formal synonym for *rich*, and it would be used more often in academic writing.

Practice

A. ***Match the words in the parentheses with their formal synonyms from the box. Then complete each sentence with the correct word.***

are fond of	charming	clever	~~former~~	pity

1. At his (past) ___*former*___ job, John was responsible for supervising other employees.
2. Police detectives have to be very (smart) __________ in order to figure out how a crime was committed.
3. The British (like) __________ drinking hot tea with milk and sugar.
4. It is difficult not to (feel sorry for) __________ those who live in difficult circumstances.
5. Peter is a very (likeable) __________ person. He has many friends because of his attractive personality.

B. ***Match the informal words with the formal synonym from the box.***

decrease	examine	increase	~~obtain~~
desire	fortunate	method	utilize

Informal	Formal
1. get	*obtain*
2. go up	
3. look at	
4. use	
5. way	
6. go down	
7. want	
8. lucky	

FROM READING TO WRITING

> ***Journal***
> Choose one of your answers and write a journal entry.

Reflecting on the Reading

Discuss the questions in pairs or small groups.

1. The narrator of the story states that "it is better to have a permanent income than to be interesting." Do you agree or disagree with this statement? Why?
2. How would you describe Oscar Wilde's writing style? Is he funny? Serious? Cheerful? Exciting? Use examples from the text to support your opinion.

PRE-READING 2

Discussion

Discuss the questions in pairs or small groups.

1. Does this story, "The Model Millionaire," interest you? Why or why not?
2. Do you like the characters? Which one?
3. How do you think the story will end? How would you like it to end?

READING 2

The Model Millionaire

Part 2

1 "Alan," said Hughie seriously, "you painters are heartless men."

2 "An artist's heart is in his head," replied Trevor; "and besides, our business is to show the world as we see it, not to make it better. And now tell me how Laura is. The old model was quite interested in her."

3 "You don't mean to say you talked to him about her?" said Hughie.

4 "Certainly I did. He knows all about the **cruel** father, the lovely Laura, and the ten thousand pounds."

5 "You told the old beggar about my private **affairs**?" cried Hughie.

6 "My dear boy," said Trevor, smiling, "that old beggar, as you call him, is one of the richest men in Europe. He could buy all London tomorrow and still have money in the bank. He has a house in every capital, eats off plates of gold, and can prevent Russia from going to war when he wishes."

7 "What on earth do you mean?" cried Hughie.

(continued)

8 "What I say," said Trevor. "The old man you saw today in my room was Baron Hausberg. He is a great friend of mine, buys all my pictures and that sort of thing, and asked me a month ago to paint him as a beggar. There's nothing surprising about that. These rich men have some strange ideas. And I must say he looked fine in those old clothes."

9 "Baron Hausberg!" cried Hughie. "Good heavens! I gave him a pound!" and he sank back into his chair in shock.

10 "Gave him a pound!" shouted Trevor and he roared with laughter. "My dear boy, you'll never see it again. His business is with other people's money."

11 "I think you ought to have told me, Alan," said Hughie in a bad temper, "and not have let me make such a fool[1] of myself."

12 "Well, to begin with, Hughie," said Trevor, "I never thought that you went about giving your money away in that careless manner. I can understand your kissing a pretty model, but not giving money to an ugly one. Besides, when you came in, I didn't know whether Hausberg would like his name mentioned. You know he wasn't in his usual dress!"

13 "How stupid he must think of me!" said Hughie.

14 "Not at all. He was in the highest **spirits** after you left, and kept laughing to himself. I couldn't understand why he was so interested in knowing all about you, but I see it all now. He'll keep your pound for you, pay you interest every six months, and have a story to tell after dinner."

[1]**fool:** a stupid person

15 "I am an unlucky devil," said Hughie. "The best thing I can do is to go to bed; and, my dear Alan, you mustn't tell anyone. I wouldn't dare[2] show my face if people knew."

16 "Nonsense! It shows your kindness of spirit, Hughie. Have another cigarette, and you can talk about Laura as much as you like."

17 But Hughie refused to stay; he walked home, feeling very unhappy, and leaving Alan Trevor helpless with laughter.

18 The next morning, as he was at breakfast, the servant brought him a card on which was written, 'Mr. Gustav Naudin, for Baron Hausberg.' "I suppose he wants me to say I am sorry about yesterday," said Hughie to himself, and he told the servant to bring the visitor in.

19 An old gentleman with gold glasses and grey hair came into the room and said, "Have I the honor of speaking to Mr. Erskine?"

20 Hughie agreed that he was Mr. Erskine.

21 "I have come from Baron Hausberg," he continued. "The Baron—"

22 "I beg[3] you, sir, that you will tell him how truly sorry I am," said Hughie quickly.

23 "The Baron," said the old gentleman with a smile, "has asked me to bring you this letter"; and he held out an envelope.

24 On the outside was written 'A wedding present to Hughie Erskine and Laura Merton, from an old beggar,' and inside was a check for ten thousand pounds.

[2]**dare:** be brave enough to do something risky, used especially in questions and negative statements

[3]**beg:** ask for something in an anxious or urgent way because you want it very much

Identifying Main Ideas

Match each description with one of the characters.

____ 1. He buys many of Trevor's paintings.

____ 2. He received ten thousand pounds from Baron Hausberg.

____ 3. He told the beggar about Hughie's life.

____ 4. He is one of the richest men in Europe.

____ 5. He wanted to know more about Hughie's life.

____ 6. He thinks Hughie is careless with his money.

____ 7. He didn't want Baron Hausberg to know about his private life.

a. Hughie Erskine	b. Alan Trevor	c. Baron Hausberg

Identifying Details

Mark the statements* T *(true) or* F *(false).

____ 1. Trevor asked Baron Hausberg if he could paint him as a beggar.

____ 2. Alan Trevor and Baron Hausberg are close friends.

____ 3. Baron Hausberg is an investment banker.

____ 4. Baron Hausberg asked Trevor not to reveal his private life to others.

Making Inferences

The answers to the questions are not stated directly in the reading. What information can be inferred to answer the questions? Work in pairs.

1. Why doesn't Hughie want people to know that he gave Baron Hausberg money?
2. Why does Alan Trevor laugh at Hughie's situation? What does this reaction suggest about Trevor's personality?
3. Look up the word *model* in a dictionary. How is Baron Hausberg both a "millionaire model" and a "model millionaire"?

FROM READING TO WRITING

Vocabulary
For more practice with vocabulary, go to page 190.

Reflecting on the Reading

Discuss the questions in pairs or small groups.

1. Did you enjoy reading "The Model Millionaire"? Why or why not?
2. Why do you think Oscar Wilde wanted to write this short story?
3. Would you read more of Oscar Wilde's stories? Explain.

WRITING

WRITING SKILL

The Thematic Analysis Essay

A **thematic analysis essay** requires writers to examine a specific theme that a story suggests. Because themes are usually implied, readers must read the story carefully to figure out what values the author is promoting and what observations he or she is making about life.

Journal
Choose one of your answers and write a journal entry.

Ask yourself these questions when writing about themes in literature:

- **Why do the characters behave as they do?** Which behaviors does the author seem to promote? Which behaviors does the author seem to be against?
- **What values do the characters have?** Are they kind? Mean? Selfish? Polite? Which values does the author seem to promote? Which values does the author seem to disagree with?
- **What effects does society have on the characters?** How does the author view the relationship between individuals and society?

Remember that authors have many choices when deciding how to portray the characters in the story and how life can affect them. Therefore, when writing a thematic analysis essay, try to understand the choices the author made and analyze the reasons why these choices were made.

Read the model essay.

MODEL

Generosity in "The Model Millionaire"

1 Although Oscar Wilde's "The Model Millionaire" is fictional, it contains a number of different themes that reflect Wilde's views on people and how they behave in the real world. Generosity is one of the topics that Wilde deals with

in the short story. The story suggests that people with money should be generous to those with little or no money.

2 The theme of generosity first emerges during a conversation between the characters of Hughie and Alan Trevor. At this point in the story, both Hughie and the reader believe that the model Trevor is painting is a poor beggar. Hughie learns that Trevor will earn two thousand pounds for the painting, but he only pays the beggar a shilling an hour for modeling. Knowing this, Hughie states, "Well, I think the model should have a share." Here Hughie is questioning Trevor's decision to pay so little to someone who is working hard and appears to be in great need of money. In this part of the story, Wilde is portraying Trevor as someone who does not care about helping the poor but should. Instead of helping the beggar, Trevor is taking advantage of him. This suggests that Wilde believes being generous to the poor is an important value.

3 Wilde continues this theme of generosity later in the story when Hughie tells Trevor that he gave the beggar a pound. Trevor is shocked at hearing this news. He says to Hughie, "I never thought that you went about giving your money away in that careless manner." This implies that Trevor believes giving the beggar any money is a mistake. Furthermore, Trevor makes fun of Hughie for being generous. Trevor's unkind treatment toward Hughie makes him an unlikable person. By making Trevor's actions unlikable, Wilde seems to be suggesting that he is not fond of people who choose not to help the poor; this in turn implies that he believes those with money should be generous to those who are less fortunate.

4 At the end of the story, the theme of generosity emerges a third time when the reader learns that Baron Hausberg gave Hughie a check for ten thousand pounds. This is a clear example of generosity. Baron Hausberg, one of the wealthiest men in Europe, is using his own money to help Hughie, who is poor. By calling Baron Hausberg the "model" millionaire, Wilde is suggesting that he is acting as a perfect model, or example, for other wealthy people. Through Baron Hausberg's actions, Wilde is again implying that the wealthy have a responsibility to help the poor.

5 In conclusion, generosity is a value that Wilde promotes in "The Model Millionaire." Treating Trevor as unlikable and Baron Hausberg as likeable shows his preference for those who have money and use it for the common good. Although this story may be one hundred years old, the themes in it can be applied to modern life as well. That is what makes "The Model Millionaire" so remarkable. It is a timeless story.

Practice

Answer the questions about the model essay.

1. Read the thesis statement again. What theme will this essay discuss?
2. What part of the story does the writer focus on in each body paragraph? Are the body paragraphs organized logically?
3. According to the author, how does Oscar Wilde portray Alan Trevor? How does the character of Alan Trevor reveal Wilde's theme? Look at paragraphs 2 and 3.
4. Why is Baron Hausberg the "model" millionaire? Look at the third body paragraph.
5. After looking at the verbs in the first body paragraph, can you identify which verb tenses writers usually use when they analyze literature?

WRITING SKILL

Organizing the Thematic Analysis Essay

Begin the introduction with an interesting observation about the story. State the author and title of the piece. Provide any necessary background information on the story, the characters, or the theme you will focus on. End with a thesis statement.

The Thesis Statement The thesis statement for a thematic analysis essay should identify the theme you will discuss. It should be your own opinion, not a fact about the story.

EXAMPLE

The story suggests that people with money should be generous to those with little or no money.

The Body Paragraphs The body paragraphs should develop your thesis statement by showing how different characters or different parts of the story support the theme.

These steps will help you organize the information in your body paragraphs:

- **Begin each body paragraph with a topic sentence that identifies the theme and the character or part of the story you will focus on.**

EXAMPLES

Topic sentence 1: The theme of generosity first emerges during a conversation between the characters of Hughie and Alan Trevor.

Topic sentence 2: Wilde continues this theme of generosity later in the story when Hughie tells Trevor that he gave the beggar a pound.

Topic sentence 3: At the end of the story, the theme of generosity emerges a third time when the reader learns that Baron Hausberg gave Hughie a check for ten thousand pounds.

- **When analyzing literature, use specific parts of the story as examples to support your ideas.** You can support your main points by paraphrasing or quoting from the text. When you **paraphrase, you summarize** a part of the story in your own words.

EXAMPLE

At this point in the story, both Hughie and the reader believe the model Trevor is painting is a poor beggar. Hughie learns that Trevor will earn two thousand pounds for the painting, but he only pays the beggar a shilling an hour for modeling.

- When you **quote, you copy** exact phrases or sentences from the story. Use quotation marks ("...") around all quotes.

EXAMPLE

Knowing this, Hughie states, "Well, I think the model should have a share."

- **After providing a paraphrase or a quote, explain how it relates to your main point.** Notice how the author of the model essay showed how Hughie's quote above relates to the theme of generosity.

EXAMPLE

Here Hughie is questioning Trevor's decision to pay so little to someone who is working hard and appears to be in great need of money. In this part of the story, Wilde is portraying Trevor as someone who does not care about helping the poor but should. Instead of helping the beggar, Trevor is taking advantage of him.

- **At the end of the body paragraph, restate the main idea of the body paragraph.**

EXAMPLE

This suggests that Wilde believes being generous to the poor is an important value.

Conclusion In your conclusion, write a restated thesis that summarizes your main points. Finish with final thoughts about the piece of literature, such as your opinion on why the theme is important or whether you agree or disagree with the author's theme.

WRITING ASSIGNMENT

Write a thematic analysis essay. Follow the steps.

STEP 1 Get ideas.

A. Choose a topic for your essay. Check (✔) it.

❑ **Topic 1:** What does Wilde suggest about being compassionate toward others? How do the characters of Hughie and Baron Hausberg support this theme? Write a thematic analysis essay on the theme of *compassion* in "The Model Millionaire."

❑ **Topic 2:** What effects does money have on the characters of Hughie, Trevor, and Baron Hausberg? What do the effects reveal about Wilde's view on the influence that money can have on people? Write a thematic analysis essay on the theme of *the power of money*.

B. Scan both parts of "The Model Millionaire" and underline parts of the story that you can use in your essay to support your main points.

STEP 2 Organize your ideas.

Make an outline for your essay. List any important supporting points, paraphrases, or quotes you plan to use in the essay.

STEP 3 Write a rough draft.

Write your essay. Use the outline from Step 2. Include vocabulary from the unit where possible.

STEP 4 Revise your rough draft.

Read your essay. Use the Writing Checklist to look for mistakes. Work alone or in pairs.

Writing Checklist

❑ Does your introduction state the author and title of the piece?

❑ Does your introduction have a clear thesis statement that identifies the theme you will discuss?

❑ Do your body paragraphs each focus on a different character or part of the story?

❑ Do they include paraphrases and/or quotes from the story to support your main points?

❑ Does your conclusion end with final thoughts?

STEP 5 Edit your writing.

A. Edit your essay. Use the correction symbols on page 173. Correct any mistakes in capitalization, punctuation, spelling, verb-tense, or the use of noun clauses.

EXAMPLE

NOUN CLAUSE

Hughie asks Trevor how much ~~does~~ he pay^s a model.

B. Work in pairs. Exchange essays and check each other's work.

STEP 6 Write a final copy.

Correct your mistakes. Copy your final essay and give it to your instructor.

Avoiding Plagiarism

Plagiarism means to pass off someone else's words or ideas as your own. In other words, it means stealing someone else's work. It happens when you use an author's ideas or copy an author's words in a paper, but you do not include his or her name. You can avoid plagiarizing the words or ideas of an author by *quoting* or *paraphrasing*.

Quoting

Quoting means using the exact same phrases or sentences from a piece of writing. To signal these words are quoted, put quotation marks " " around them. If the quote does not start the sentence, put a comma before the first quotation mark. Always place the concluding period or question mark inside the second quotation mark.

EXAMPLE

According to Davies, "The right to privacy is the right to protect ourselves against intrusion from the outside world."

Below are a few different ways to introduce a quote. Be sure to always include the author's last name.

- **According to** Davies, "..."
- Davies **says**, "..."
- Davies **states**, "..."

Paraphrasing

Paraphrasing means taking one or more sentences from a reading, and writing the same ideas, but in your own words. Here are a few general rules to follow when paraphrasing.

- Include the author's last name.
- Make your paraphrase about the same length as the original quote.
- Make sure that your paraphrase sounds different from the original.
- Don't change the meaning in the original quote. *Same idea, different words.*

Here are some ways to state the same idea using different words:

- Change the words and wording as much as possible by using synonyms.
- Use different forms of the same word (adjective, noun, verb, adverb).
- Try to put the ideas from the quote in a different order in your paraphrase.

Read the following quote. Compare the quote to the incorrect and correct paraphrases.

QUOTE

"The widespread adoption of tracking won't be done against our will but initially with our consent," says Davies.

INCORRECT PARAPHRASE

According to Davies, the widespread use of tracking won't be done against our wishes but with our approval.

CORRECT PARAPHRASE

According to Davies, people won't object to the use of tracking when it becomes prevalent; in the beginning, people will accept it.

The first paraphrase is incorrect because it is too similar to the original quote. Many words are repeated, so the sentence sounds almost the same as the original. In the correct paraphrase, the sentences sound very different, but the idea has remained the same. The correct paraphrase uses synonyms and different wording to state the same idea. This chart shows the original words and how they were replaced in the paraphrase.

ORIGINAL WORDING	PARAPHRASE
widespread	prevalent
the adoption of tracking	the use of tracking
won't be done against our will	people won't object to
initially	in the beginning
with our consent	people will accept it

Practice

Circle the letter of the best paraphrase for each quote.

1. According to Davies, "The right to privacy is the right to protect ourselves against intrusion from the outside world."
   a. According to Davies, the right to privacy is the right to defend ourselves against intrusions from the outside.
   b. According to Davies, the right to protect ourselves against intrusion from the world is the right to privacy.
   c. According to Davies, everyone has the right to stop the outside world from invading his or her privacy.
2. Levy believes that "sooner or later . . . we will realize that information taken from our movements has compromised our 'locational privacy.'"
   a. Sooner or later, people will figure out that information taken from their movements has compromised their "locational privacy," according to Levy.
   b. People will eventually see that their "locational privacy" has been threatened by the collection of data about their movements, according to Levy.
   c. According to Levy, we will realize that information taken from our movements has compromised our "locational privacy"—sooner or later.
3. "In a majority of countries, employers are permitted—'within reason'—to place all employees under constant surveillance," says Davies.
   a. Within reason, employers are permitted to place all workers under constant surveillance in a majority of countries, says Davies.
   b. Businesses are allowed to keep track of their workers in most countries around the world, says Davies.
   c. In a majority of countries, employers are allowed to put all their employees under constant surveillance, says Davies.

Grammar Reference

SENTENCE TYPES

Simple Sentences

Type 1 With one subject and one verb

S + V Sam works.

Type 2 With more than one subject and a verb

S + S + V Sam and Helen work.

Type 3 With one subject and more than one verb

S + V + V Sam works and plays.

Type 4 With more than one subject and more than one verb

S + S + V + V Sam and Helen work and play.

Compound Sentences

Type 1 With a comma and a coordinating conjunction

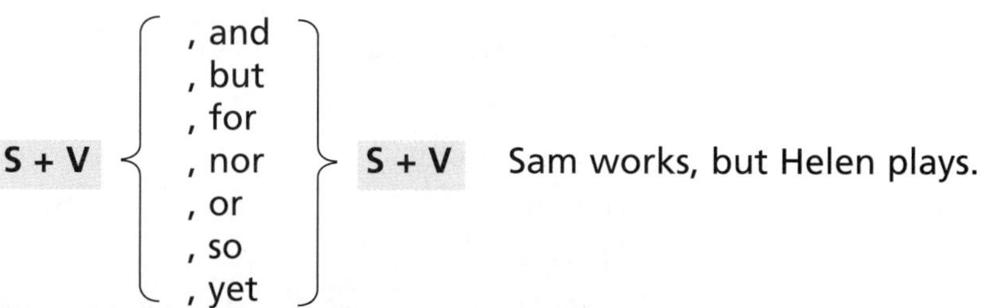

Type 2 With a semicolon

S + V ; **S + V** Sam works; Helen plays.

Type 3 With a semicolon and a transition followed by a comma

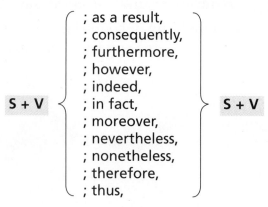

S + V { ; as a result, / ; consequently, / ; furthermore, / ; however, / ; indeed, / ; in fact, / ; moreover, / ; nevertheless, / ; nonetheless, / ; therefore, / ; thus, } **S + V**

Complex Sentences

TYPE 1 With a subordinating conjunction midsentence

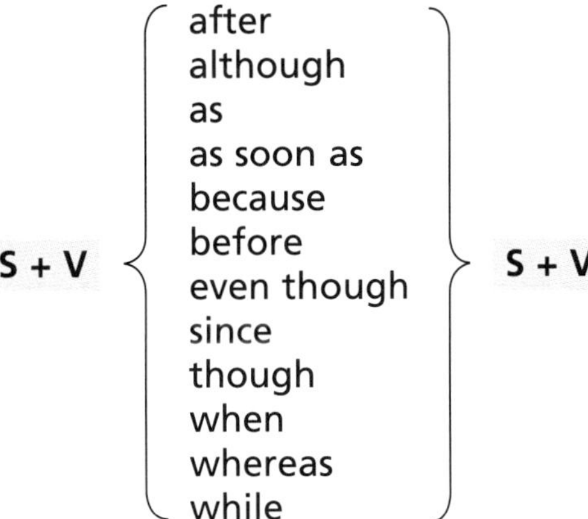

TYPE 2 With an initial subordinating conjunction (often with a comma after the initial clause)

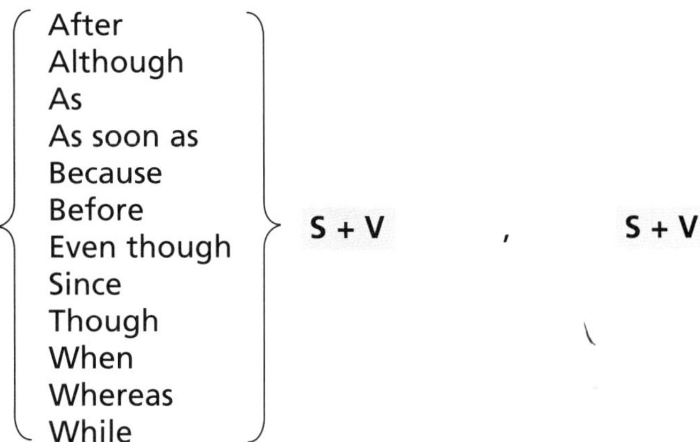

TRANSITIONS AND CONNECTORS

	TRANSITION SIGNALS	COORDINATING CONJUNCTIONS	SUBORDINATING CONJUNCTIONS
To give an **additional idea**	also, in addition, moreover,	, and	—
To show **direct contrast**	however, in contrast, on the other hand,	, but	while whereas
To show **unexpected contrast**	nevertheless, nonetheless,	, yet	although even though though
To show **cause**	—	, for	because since
To show **effect**	as a result, consequently, for this reason, therefore, thus,	, so	—
To show **similarity**	in addition, likewise, similarly	, and	—
To show **time relationships**	after that, before that, later, then	—	before after when while as as soon as since

Correction Symbols

SYMBOL	MEANING	EXAMPLE
a/p	active/passive error	*a/p* The house **located** on a busy street.
art	wrong article or missing article	*art* I read **book** yesterday.
agr	subject-verb agreement error	*agr* Mr. Schmidt **listen** to music in his car.
E	not an English word	*E* Anna wanted to go to school, **pero** she was sick.
nn	not necessary	*nn* My professor lives in **the** Chicago.
P	punctuation error	*P* You're right**,** I should study harder.
s	subject missing	*s* **Is** not easy to speak in English on the telephone.
sp.	spelling error	*sp.* This is an **exampul** of a spelling error.
s/p	singular/plural error	*s/p* There are many **student** in my class.
v	verb missing	*v* **I from** China.
v.t.	verb tense error	*v.t.* I **drive** my car to work last night.
wf	wrong form of word	*wf* He always walks very **quick**.
pp	wrong preposition or missing preposition	*pp* The children should not play **on** the house.
ww	wrong word	*ww* She **said** me to go home.
/	lower-case	We went to the Park on a sunny Day.
≡	upper-case	my classes end on may 15.
○	missing word	My mother needs to **go the** doctor.
∼	reverse word order	I enjoy spending time with my **friends good**.

Vocabulary Review

UNIT 1

Reading 1

Circle the best word in each pair to complete the sentences.

1. Sir Sandford Fleming was a **prominent / uniform** man in Canada because he helped build the country's first major railway system.
2. Many railway companies **implemented / took into account** the use of time zones in 1884 even though no country had officially adopted the zones at that time.
3. Fleming's original plan **fostered / incorporated** the idea of four separate time zones.
4. Fleming's time zones have had **underlying / extensive** influence in the world. All countries base their time on his twenty-four time zones.
5. Fleming created a(n) **systematic / underlying** method for people to know what time it is all over the world.
6. Because of Fleming's plan, travelers can know train schedules in advance. **Nevertheless / As a result**, a traveler may have to wait for a train if one has just left.
7. A single, **uniform / prominent** way of telling time is especially important now that people travel around the globe.

Reading 2

Complete the paragraph with the correct words in the box. One word is not used.

captivated	exceeded	reluctant	trend
commonplace	persistent	revolutionary	triggered

Birdseye was so successful largely because of his personality. He was a creative and (1) _______________ person. His invention of frozen food was truly (2) _______________. In fact, it not only changed how people make food at home, but it also (3) _______________ a major change in the restaurant industry. At first, many chefs were (4) _______________ to use frozen food in their dishes because they worried they wouldn't taste as good. Today, however, the use of frozen food has become (5) _______________ in restaurant kitchens around the world. Although many people thought frozen foods would only be a (6) _______________, history has shown that they are here to stay. If Birdseye were still alive today, it is safe to say that he would find that the success of his invention has (7) _______________ his expectations.

Reading 1

Read the sentences. Replace each boldfaced word with its synonym in the box. One word is not used.

approach	contacts	~~initiative~~	potential
are relevant to	further	keep in mind	source

1. Companies look for employees who can take the ~~**lead**~~ *initiative* in getting projects started and finished in a timely manner.
2. When you apply for a job, it is a good idea to check that your education and experience **are related to** the position.
3. Stefanie has found two **possible** jobs in today's newspaper, both of which match her educational and work experience.
4. When looking for a job, it is important to **remember** that who you know is as important as what you know.
5. There are many business schools that allow people to **improve** their job-related computer skills.
6. Looking through a newspaper's classified ads is a popular **method** people use to find a job.
7. Career experts have found that fewer than half of all jobs are advertised. Instead, people find out about those jobs through their personal **connections**.

Reading 2

Complete the article with the words in the box.

accomplishments	entrepreneur	turn into
came up with	operates	was vital to

Oprah Winfrey

Many people think of Oprah Winfrey as a celebrity, but she is also a very successful (1) _______________. Winfrey is worth more than $1.5 billion. She (2) _______________ her own television production company, and she publishes two of her own magazines. Her life today, however, is very different from her childhood. How did this poor girl (3) _______________ one of the richest women in America? Knowing that a good education (4) _______________ success, Winfrey's grandmother taught her to read at age three. From that point on, Winfrey never stopped learning.

One of Winfrey's earliest (5) _______________ was becoming the youngest person ever to do television news, at age nineteen. Eventually, Winfrey (6) _______________ the idea of The Oprah Winfrey Show, which has become one of the most popular talk shows in television history. Today, Winfrey has become one of the richest and most generous women in America.

Reading 1

Complete the paragraph with the words in the box. One word is not used.

demand	dramatic	objective
diminish	impact	points out

In "Can Cell-Phone Recycling Help African Gorillas?" author Stefan Lovgren (1) _______________ that recycling cell phones could help save gorilla populations in the Congo. Today, people are killing the gorillas in their search for coltan, which is used in cell phones. American zoos have begun cell-phone recycling programs to lessen the world's (2) _______________ for new phones, which they hope will (3) _______________ the amount of coltan taken from the Congo. Most importantly, zoos hope their recycling programs will have a positive (4) _______________ on the gorillas and help meet the zoos' main (5) _______________: to put an end to this situation and let the gorillas live in peace.

Reading 2

Circle the best word or words to complete the sentences.

1. Humans have **accumulated / exploited** many of the earth's underground oil reserves.
2. People's **consumption / scarcity** of oil continues to grow because of the increasing number of cars on the road.
3. Some scientists believe there won't be enough oil to **exploit / sustain** global demands in the future.
4. Many scientists are looking for **alternative / finite** fuels so people won't have to use oil for energy.
5. **The prospect of / The recognition of** getting water from underground aquifers is exciting not only to scientists, but to all who care about our planet.
6. Many of Earth's resources, such as water and oil, are **finite / alternative** and therefore should be conserved and used with care.
7. Water **security / scarcity** is an important issue that needs to be resolved for future generations.

Reading 1

Complete the sentences with the words in the box.

associate with	judgment	raises the question
attempts	odds	superstition

1. Walking under a ladder is an action that some people ____________ bad luck.
2. Students who carry good luck charms to an exam believe they will improve their ____________ of passing the test.
3. The idea that Friday the 13th is an unlucky day is a ____________ that many Americans have.
4. Athletes have made many ____________ to win games by carrying their favorite good luck charms with them.
5. Superstitions can help people feel in control, but this ____________: why do we need to feel in control?
6. Everyone must make his or her own ____________ about the power of superstitions.

Reading 2

Rewrite the sentences. Replace the underlined word(s) with the best word or phrase in the box.

conclusive	denied	is confined to
controversy	extraordinary	

1. Nessie <u>is only found in</u> Loch Ness, a large lake in Scotland.

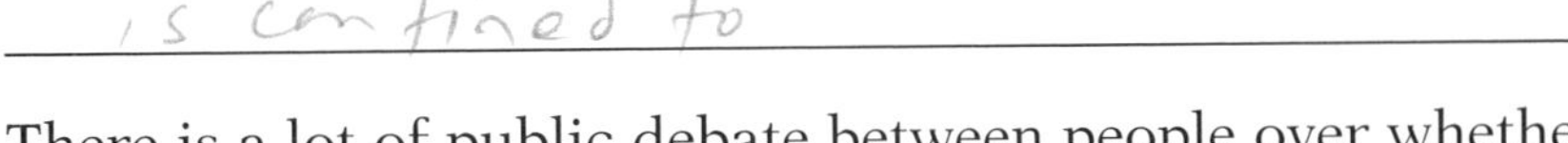

is confined to

2. There is a lot of <u>public debate between people</u> over whether Bigfoot is real.

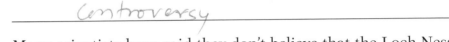

controversy

3. Many scientists have <u>said they don't believe</u> that the Loch Ness Monster exists.

denied

4. Cryptologists are scientists who study <u>very unusual</u> creatures.

extraordinary

5. Many scientists won't believe in Bigfoot without <u>definite</u> proof.

conclusive.

Reading 1

Complete the paragraph with the words in the box.

accounted for	complemented	hypothesis	revealed
categorized	distinct	overlap	tended to

In "Musical Personalities," the author outlines four (1) _______________ personalities based on the music people listen to. Psychologists Peter J. Rentfrow and Samuel D. Gosling tested their (2) _______________ about musical personalities by researching undergraduate students, and their study (3) _______________ some interesting results. The psychologists (4) _______________ listeners of blues, folk, jazz, and classical music as Reflective and Complex. People with an Intense and Rebellious personality preferred rock and heavy metal, and they (5) _______________ be risk-takers. The Upbeat and Conventional were social and liked pop and country music. Finally, the high-energy music of rap, funk, and dance (6) _______________ those with an Energetic and Rhythmic personality. These four categories (7) _______________ most people, but Rentfrow and Gosling noticed that there was some (8) _______________ between the personalities as well.

Reading 2

Read the sentences. Replace each boldfaced word with its synonym in the box.

adapt to	confirm	enhance	excessive
circumstances	encounter	ensure	predominantly

1. When people begin a new job, it is common for them to **experience** some difficulties at first. It can take some time for them to **get used to** their new environment.
2. In order to **show** a hypothesis **is correct**, scientists often have to examine the same subject under different **conditions** to see if their theory holds true.
3. **Too much** work and not enough sleep can make people feel more stress. In contrast, eating right and exercising can **improve** our mood and decrease feelings of stress and depression.
4. At a company, it is **mainly** the boss's responsibility to **make sure** that his employees are not overstressed by the amount of work they have to do.

Reading I

Read the sentences. Replace each boldfaced word with its synonym in the box.

are inclined to	constitute	emerge	mentality
common	contrary to	fundamental	remarkable

1. **In contrast to** popular belief, women buy almost as many electronics as men do.
2. Many men have the **attitude** of a hunter when they go shopping.
3. Men **are likely to** purchase an item without asking anyone for advice.
4. Men and women today seem to have a **similar** interest in buying electronics online.
5. American men's emphasis on independence and aggression is the **basic** reason behind their risk-taking behavior.
6. Women **represent** about half of all workers in the United States today.
7. When comparing men's and women's shopping habits, many differences **begin to appear**.
8. The Internet has caused **surprising** and unpredicted changes in people's shopping habits.

Reading 2

Circle the best word in each pair to complete the sentences.

1. Men's use of cosmetics today is not a new **phenomenon / assumption**. Men have used cosmetics for thousands of years.
2. Some of today's cosmetics **comprise / interact with** the same ingredients that the Egyptians used thousands of years ago.
3. It is a common **stereotype / version** that men don't care much about their looks.
4. Today's more **liberal / various** young people don't believe there is only one definition of masculinity. To them, it can have **liberal / various** definitions.
5. A number of companies now sell organic **versions / assumptions** of skin care products that are believed to be safer and more "natural."
6. Many **assumptions / versions** about the use of cosmetics are based on stereotypes and are, therefore, not true.
7. As more and more cultures **intervene between / interact with** one another, beliefs about cosmetics will continue to change.

Reading I

Complete the paragraph with the words in the box. One word is not used.

activates	evolved	phase	subconscious
bond	innate	sense	undergo

In "Why You Can't Turn Away," Richard Conniff discusses the reasons why people watch, and continue to watch, disturbing events. Scientists believe humans have a(n) (1) ______________ capacity to feel other people's emotions. For instance, when we see an accident, we feel a(n) (2) ______________ of fear just as the victim does. We (3) ______________ this same reaction when we watch disasters on television. The brain remembers the connections between these events and feelings, and they are stored in our (4) ______________ mind until we need them. When a disaster occurs, the brain (5) ______________ the memory of these events, which helps us be better prepared to deal with the problem. Scientists believe that our ability to feel a(n) (6) ______________ with people in danger (7) ______________ because it helped early humans survive, and this still occurs today whether we see the danger with our own eyes or on television.

Reading 2

Circle the best word in each pair to complete the sentences.

1. Looking at people in the eyes while they are talking to you **assures / attributes to** them that you are listening closely.
2. Social problems often **facilitate / stem from** economic problems. Crime, for instance, can often be **attributed to / promoted to** poverty.
3. Working **collaboratively / ultimately** requires people to listen to one another's ideas and solve problems as a group.
4. Living in a college dorm **stems from / facilitates** more interaction between students. As a result, dorm life **assures / promotes** a sense of community among the students who live there.
5. **No matter / In fact** how much humans value independence, we all need to cooperate to survive.
6. There are many reasons to explain why people laugh, but **ultimately / collaboratively**, people laugh because it feels good.

Reading 1

Read the sentences. Replace the boldfaced word(s) with a synonym in the box.

compromises	drawbacks	pursuing
consent	monitor	verify

1. At the airport, transportation authorities use security cameras to **carefully watch** what travelers are doing.
2. The police have been **looking for** the criminal all day. He is a suspect in a robbery.
3. Supporters of employee tracking do not believe the technology **puts** people's privacy **at risk**.
4. Many people feel that companies should not read their employees' e-mails without their **permission**.
5. Because he was traveling overseas in a month, John had to **check** that his passport was still up-to-date.
6. Tracking technology can be very helpful, but it has some **disadvantages** as well.

Reading 2

Complete the sentences with the best word(s) in the box.

are linked to	expanded	transmit
convinced	invasive	trustworthy

Believe it or not, security cameras may no longer be found only on Earth. Some of today's newest satellites in space can actually take close-up pictures of Earth. For now, the data that satellites (1) _______________ back to Earth is used for good purposes. Many people use satellite images to map farmland and forests, but their use has (2) _______________ to mapping cities as well. Today, these images (3) _______________ websites for the general public to see.

Although privately-owned satellite cameras seem very beneficial, some worry that they could become too (4) _______________ if they are used as security cameras. Others are (5) _______________ that the images could fall into the wrong person's hands, especially into the hands of someone who is not (6) _______________ and might use the images in a harmful way.

Readings 1 & 2

Complete the sentences with the words in the box.

charming	cruel	is fond of	pitied
clever	former	miserable	spirits

1. Alan Trevor ________________ Hughie because he is a very ________________ and cheerful person.
2. Hughie has no job at the present. His ________________ jobs included being a stock trader, a tea trader, and a wine seller.
3. Alan Trevor is friends with Hughie because he is "beautiful and stupid." In other words, he thinks Hughie is good-looking, but not very ________________.
4. Hughie ________________ the beggar because he looked so ________________ in his old torn clothes.
5. Baron Hausberg was in good ________________ after Hughie gave him a pound.
6. Alan Trevor is ________________ to laugh at Hughie for giving away his last pound.

Target Vocabulary

*Coxhead's *Academic Word List (2000)*
**Dilin Liu's *The Most Frequently Used American English Idioms* (2003)

UNIT 1

Reading 1

extensive
foster
implement*
incorporate*
nonetheless*
prominent
systematic
take into account**
underlying*
uniform*

Reading 2

alteration*
captivate
commence*
commonplace
exceed*
persistent*
reluctant*
revolutionary*
trend*
trigger*

UNIT 2

Reading 1

acquaintance
approach*
be relevant to*
contact*
further
get in touch with**
initiative*
keep in mind**
potential*
source*

Reading 2

accomplishment
be vital to
come up with**
entrepreneur
expertise*
operate
practical
turn into**

UNIT 3

Reading 1

contribute to*
demand
diminish*
dramatic*
highlight*
ideal
impact*
objective*
point out**

Reading 2

accumulate*
alternative*
consumption*
exploit*
finite*
scarcity
sustain*
the prospect of*

UNIT 4

Reading 1

associate with
attempt
judgment
odds*
raise the question
superstition

Reading 2

be confined to*
be related to
conclusive*
controversy*
deny*
extraordinary

UNIT 5

Reading 1

account for
categorize
complement*
distinct*
extroverted
hypothesis*
interaction*
overlap*
reveal*
tend to

Reading 2

- adapt to*
- circumstances*
- confirm*
- encounter*
- enhance*
- ensure*
- excessive
- predominantly*

UNIT 6

Reading 1

- accordingly
- be inclined to*
- common
- constitute*
- contrary to*
- emerge*
- fundamental*
- mentality*
- remarkable

Reading 2

- assumption*
- comprise*
- interact with*
- liberal*
- phenomenon*
- stereotype
- various
- version*

UNIT 7

Reading 1

- activate
- bond*
- conscious
- evolve*
- innate
- phase*
- role*
- sense
- subconscious
- undergo*

Reading 2

- assure*
- attribute to*
- collaboratively
- facilitate*
- no matter**
- promote*
- stem from
- ultimately*

UNIT 8

Reading 1

- be based on
- be devoted to*
- compromise
- consent*
- drawback
- exception
- monitor*
- pursue*
- verify

Reading 2

- be linked to*
- convinced*
- dilemma
- expand*
- in this case
- invasive
- technique*
- transmit*
- trustworthy

UNIT 9

Reading 1

- astonishing
- be fond of
- charming
- clever
- former
- miserable
- pity

Reading 2

- affairs
- cruel
- spirits

Credits

Photo Credits: Cover: Cloud Nine Productions/Corbis; **Page 1** (left) Shutterstock, (right) Shutterstock; **Page 21** Shutterstock; **Page 39** AFP/Getty Images; **Page 59** (left) Shutterstock, (right) iStockphoto; **Page 73** Shutterstock; **Page 93** Shutterstock; **Page 112** Shutterstock; **Page 131** Superstock; **Page 150** Shutterstock.

Text Credits: Page 30 "How to Run a Successful Business" from *Career World*, November, 2000. Special permission granted by *Weekly Reader*, published and copyrighted by Weekly Reader Corporation. All rights reserved. **Page 41** "Can Cell-Phone Recycling Help African Gorillas?" Reprinted with the permission of Stefan Lovgren/National Geographic Image Collection. **Page 62** "Lucky Charms" Used by permission of the *Times Union*, Albany, NY. **Page 114** "Why You Can't Turn Away" by Richard Conniff © 2005. Reprinted by permission. **Page 133** "Future with Nowhere to Hide" from *Newsweek* issue 6/7/2007. Reprinted with permission. **Page 140** "More Parents Going High-Tech to Track Kids" The Associated Press, September, 2005. Reprinted by permission. **Pages 152, 157** "The Model Millionaire" from *Outstanding Short Stories* (Penguin Readers) by G. C. Thornley. Reprinted by permission of Pearson Education Limited.

Index

Writing

Writing Skills

Mechanics

Grammar

Readings

Reading Skills